ENTERTAINING
IN THE
VICTORIAN STYLE

ENTERTAINING
IN THE
VICTORIAN STYLE

REFRESHMENTS • SETTINGS • EVENTS

MARILYN HANSEN

DUTTON STUDIO BOOKS

NEW YORK

DUTTON STUDIO BOOKS
Published by the Penguin Group
Penguin Books USA Inc.,
375 Hudson Street,
New York, New York, 10014, U.S.A.
Penguin Books Ltd,
27 Wrights Lane,
London W8 5TZ, England
Penguin Books Australia Ltd,
Ringwood, Victoria, Australia
Penguin Books Canada Ltd,
2801 John Street,
Markham, Ontario,
Canada L3R 1B4
Penguin Books (N.Z.) Ltd,
192–190 Wairau Road,
Auckland 10, New Zealand

Penguin Books Ltd, Registered Offices:
Harmondsworth, Middlesex, England

First published by Dutton Studio Books, an imprint of
Penguin Books USA Inc.

First printing, October, 1990
10   9   8   7   6   5   4   3   2

Library of Congress Catalogue Card Number: 90-80861
ISBN: 0-525-24913-3

"The Ladies' " Blackberry Shrub from *Sumptuous Dining in
Gaslight San Francisco* by Frances DeTalavera Berger and
John Parke Custis, copyright © 1985 by Frances DeTalavera
Berger and John Parke Custis. Used by permission of
Doubleday, a division of Bantam Doubleday Dell Publishing
Group.

ENTERTAINING IN THE VICTORIAN STYLE
was conceived and produced by Running Heads Incorporated,
55 West 21st Street,
New York, NY 10010

Editor: Sarah Kirshner
Designer: Lesley Ehlers
Managing Editor: Lindsey Crittenden
Production Manager: Linda Winters
Photo Editor: Ellie Watson

Set in Simoncini Garamond
Typeset by David E. Seham Associates Inc.
Color separations by Hong Kong Scanner Craft Company Ltd.
Printed and bound in Singapore by Times Offset Pte Ltd.

To my parents Elsie Edith Williams Sjogren and Clarence LeGrand Sjogren, who originally inspired me with the joys and pleasures of entertaining, and my daughters Carla Jane Hansen and Ava Marilyn Hansen, who have both tasted and listened to the evolving chapters.

Many people contributed generously to this book. I would especially like to thank the staff at Running Heads: Marta Hallett for giving me the opportunity to write this book; my editor, Sarah Kirshner, whose steadfast vision was inspiring and supportive throughout the project; Ellie Watson for her energetic and enthusiastic pursuit of photographic excellence; Linda Greer for her dedicated and thorough work on the recipes, and all others who saw the book through production. Thanks also to Lesley Ehlers for her elegant design in the Victorian spirit. Cyril Nelson at Dutton provided expert advice. Patricia Godfrey and Jill Benz helped with preparation of the manuscript. Thanks also to all the photographers whose work makes this book so beautiful, particularly Tony Giammarino, Dennis Krukowski, and Esther and Franklin Schmidt.

I'm grateful to the following individuals for their help and advice: The Basquetrie, Columbia, MO; Alma Demarest, New York, NY; Michelle Erceg, Saratoga Springs, NY; Karen Blatnik and Martha Craig, Fitz & Floyd, Dallas, TX; Sal DiFlorio and Brian Gallo, The Inn at Fernbrook, Centerville, MA; Donna and Robert Taylor and Vera Howell, Grace Place Inn, Greenwood, SC; Connie Emery, Haderway House, Lancaster, KS; Alan Kraus, Hudson Street Papers, New York, NY; Joe and Margi Hemingway, Hemingway Associates, Brooklyn, NY; Inger of Sweden, New York, NY; Elizabeth Keihm, M. M. Fenner Company, New York, NY; Alan Churchill and Tom Clark, The Mansion, Rock City Falls, NY; Marilyn Farrell-Reed, Saratoga Springs, NY; Ray Carucci and Marie Vitalo, The Secret Ingredient, Hoboken, NJ; Marion Kukliewicz, Victorian Visions, Turners Falls, MA; John and Cile Burbidge, Danvers, MA; The House of Seven Gables, Salem, MA; Cheryl Weatherly Schultz, Dallas, TX; Cheryl Kleinman, New York, NY; Anne Jenkins and Nancy Watson, Service Service, Chicago, IL; Gloria Gale, Overland Park, KS.

I would also like to thank all of those who have been so supportive in this and other efforts: Barbara Kafka, Zack Hanle, Anita Fial, and my sister and brother-in-law, Doris and Fred Rowe.

CONTENTS

INTRODUCTION

$\mathcal{Q}$UEEN VICTORIA HAS GIVEN HER NAME TO A PERIOD IN WHICH ENTERTAINING, AT HOME AND IN PUBLIC, REACHED HEIGHTS OF SPLENDOR. AS IN SO MANY MATTERS OF STYLE IN THE SIXTY-THREE YEARS OF HER REIGN (1837 TO 1901), IN MODES OF ENTERTAINING THE BRITISH TOOK THE LEAD AND THE AMERICANS FOLLOWED. WEALTHY AMERICANS ASPIRED TO THE GENTEEL, CULTIVATED WAY OF LIFE REPRESENTED BY THE BRITISH AND EUROPEAN UPPER CLASSES. PRESIDENT JAMES BUCHANAN WAS NO DIFFERENT AND, IN FACT, ENGINEERED ONE OF THE GREAT AMERICAN SOCIAL EVENTS OF THE MID-NINETEENTH CENTURY BY INVITING ALBERT EDWARD, PRINCE OF WALES, TO VISIT THE UNITED STATES IN 1860 AFTER HIS TRIP TO CANADA. BUCHANAN

called upon the talents of Gautier, a French caterer who had a spectacular way with partridge, terrapin, oysters, lobster, and wild turkey, to prepare two lavish dinner parties for the debonair nineteen-year-old Crown Prince (later to become King Edward VII), sending Washington hostesses into a state of competitive frenzy.

Americans emulated, if not exceeded, the British in feats of culinary consumption and excess in the Victorian period. The same chef, Gautier, had prepared a breathtaking feast for Buchanan's Inaugural Ball in March 1857. Five thousand guests were served eighty rounds of beef, seventy-five hams, sixty saddles of mutton, four saddles of venison, four hundred gallons of oysters, five hundred quarts of chicken salad, one hundred and twenty-five tongues, five hundred quarts of jellies, pâtés of all description, and twelve hundred quarts of various flavors of ice cream. The meal was capped by a splendid pyramid cake, four feet high and decorated with the insignias of the thirty-one states in the Union.

The privations of the Civil War not too many years later certainly dampened the American desire for such celebratory feasts, but as the century continued, the rise of industry in Europe and America created a well-to-do class of people who lavished time and attention on the niceties of entertaining at home. It was the home, with structured dining and social rituals, that sheltered the family and its private circle from the seemingly relentless demands of the outside world. The dining room itself became the center of family life all during the Victorian era.

As Susan Williams writes in *Savory Suppers and Fashionable Feasts: Dining in America* (1985):

> "Meals along the entire spectrum of [social] means . . . were linked by a common concern with ritual, formality and schedule. The times at which people ate, the procedures they followed for serving and eating foods, the ways they felt were necessary and proper to dress for meals, the type of environment in which food should be consumed, the kinds of social arrangements for the table—who should sit where, what one should say and how one should say it, who should speak to whom—even the food itself were, in effect, canonized by the end of the nineteenth century . . ."

For example, the standard times to eat breakfast, lunch, and dinner changed during the period. Dinner was usually the main meal served in the middle of the day. However, as man's work moved into the city for business, it became impractical to return home for midday dinner, so dinner came at the end of the day. On the farm of course, where chores started early in the day, the practice of having the main meal in the middle of the day persisted for many years.

To define a social structure, to make a hierarchy of class, to separate those who "have" and therefore "know" how to conduct themselves socially, an elaborate code of etiquette was demanded by the social arbiters. Books and magazine articles were written to give direction and description of proper etiquette, or deportment, as it was called then. For example, etiquette books such as *Our Deportment or The Manners, Conduct and Dress of the Most Refined Society* by John H. Young, A. M. and *Decorum: A Practical Treatise on Etiquette and Dress of the Best American Society* by John A. Ruth, and magazines such as *The Woman's Home Companion, Peters-*

An elegant Victorian parlor poised for entertaining, below. The elaborately carved marble mantel-piece is topped with a gilt mirror. A dried floral arrangement under glass and fresh fruit in a raised pedestal bowl add the right touch.

A formal dining room in Rochester, New York, above, has windows decorated with tasseled valences, a needlepoint tablecloth with tassels, and pressed flowers framed on the wall. Flowers also grace the table under glass.

on's *Ladies National Magazine, Godey's Lady's Book,* and the *Ladies' Home Journal,* gave detailed information on correct manners, menus, and dining.

Social occasions were opportunities to display one's wealth and position in society. Invitations to attend parties and events of all kinds, as well as the giving of such entertainments, were indications of one's social standing.

Being invited to a tea by a person of a certain status was important, as was attending and demonstrating correct behavior there. Needless to say, formal dinners were on an even higher social level. The host and hostess had the opportunity to invite whomever they chose, create a menu, present the proper serving of it along with appropriate table decorations.

It was a highly social time with entertaining, conspicuous consumption, and display of wealth among the most important motivating forces of the era. From breakfasts to teas, croquet parties to fancy dress balls—entertaining reigned supreme and being invited to such events assured one's social desirability.

It is primarily the upper- and middle-class Victorian home, its routines, and its celebrations that this book examines. We describe historic Victorian social events, give menus for Victorian-style entertainments, suggestions for decor and special accents, and recipes for Victorian dishes adapted to modern kitchens. At first, you may find Victorian food and decor a bit rich for your taste, but keep in mind that if there was excess, it was because there was plenty. Victorian recipes contain ample amounts of cream and butter; nineteenth-century cooks liberally covered pies, cakes, and their renowned shortcakes with whipped cream because farms were producing dairy products in abundance. In the expanding United States, there was a seemingly unending supply of fish, game, and land. And it was all free to be had for everyone, at least the healthy and ·adventurous, not just for the upper classes. With plenty came inventive cooks and all manner of reasons to feast and entertain.

In our age of calorie- and cholesterol-counting, what (besides potential pounds) is to be gained from learning about Victorian modes of entertaining? Surely excess is to be avoided, but abundance and variety in food and the appreciation of good eating and good cooking are values worth holding on to. Similarly, though many Victorian mores and modes of social behavior are not applicable to late twentieth-century lives, we still yearn for something from this earlier age.

Certainly many of our forebears were not wealthy participants in the grand Victorian social scheme as it is described in this book, but they were part of its workings and aspired to its ideals. My own paternal grandmother was, like so many Americans, an immigrant to the United States. Hilma Johannsen Sjogren was employed by a well-to-do New York City family in the late 1880s. Hilma had come from Sweden and was the family cook; when the owners went to their summer house, she and my grandfather, Alexander, were live-in caretakers of the family brownstone. Hilma, who often said "I would rather give a dinner party than have a new dress," took advantage of the family's absence to invite her *own* friends to a dinner party in her employers' dining room. After Hilma and Alexander cooked an elaborate dinner and served it, using the home's fine china and silver, Hilma would regally rise from the table and recite poetry to amuse the assembled

This Victorian-styled dining room in Rochester, New York, below, has a coffered ceiling and a chandelier with flame-shaped bulbs. A carved marble fireplace and mirror are the focal points at the end of the room.

guests. Like the spirited and energetic Hilma, perhaps we can picture ourselves presenting a fine, cultivated Victorian-style dinner for our own friends, and just as Hilma borrowed the best china for the evening, we can "borrow" the best customs of Victorian entertaining.

Much of the appeal of this past culture is due in no little part to our desire to live with more beauty and less harsh reality, more predictability, more order, and infinitely more graciousness. "Progress" in the ensuing years since the Victorian era has not solved all of society's problems. Consequently, in our personal realm we want to have some kind of control and preserve our sense of family even though traditional family structures have changed. We still want values of tradition and manners and good behavior in our children. We too want beauty and order in our sometimes frantic lives. It is this pervasive desire for a solid past and a stable future that brings us to the door of our grandparents and Victorian times to appreciate and incorporate the best from the experiences of those who successfully came before.

The structure of the day itself, with meals at their proper times, gave predictability to the Victorian day. The creation and maintenance of a proper, well-run, aesthetically beautiful home was a highly esteemed value in the Golden Era. Might we not benefit significantly ourselves from bringing some semblance of order into our busy lives? We crave a nourishing breakfast in a serene environment, a leisurely brunch on Sunday, invitations, dressing up, celebrations, gala dinners, and soothing tea time. We are enthusiastic about antiques, ornate silver, rose-covered china, marble, lace, and potpourri. Yes, we want to enjoy and we want comfort. Where to find it but in an earlier, robust age in which people were not timid about decorating; dressing up; being surrounded by bright colors and lush plants and flowers; and serving rich, varied, and wonderful foods in a parade of decorative courses. We know all too well that we can't "have it all," but we also know that we deserve a rich, full lifestyle, and we are not about to be denied. What's more, it's fun to go back and weave some of these charming old customs into our own lives, bombarded as we are with messages about status and image. The Victorians didn't concern themselves with image; they were concerned about being the genuine thing. We are looking for, and hoping to find, some of the proven, solid substance that will sustain us for the days ahead.

We can indeed create and capture some of this essence for ourselves, especially in our own homes and in entertaining others. What greater compliment than to open your heart and share your home and table, catching the spirit of the season and the glory of the hour?

An ornate lamp, above, originally kerosene but now electric, is on a side table arranged for stereopticon viewing, with a dried bouquet featuring honesty and eucalyptus. A contemporary Rochester home, right, vividly shows the Victorian love of ornamentation.

A Note to the Reader on the Recipes:

This book includes sixteen menus for Victorian-style events that you might wish to duplicate in your own home. We have endeavored to give the reader a sense of the Victorian diet and the variety of courses and dishes served at many of these events. Where possible, we have adapted authentic menus to include types of food the modern reader might wish to re-create in his or her own kitchen. We have chosen a few dishes from each of these historic menus that we thought might pique the reader's culinary interest and we have included the complete recipe for these foods. We have tried to give a comprehensive selection of main dishes, appetizers, beverages, vegetables dishes and, of course, desserts. Many of the dishes for which we have *not* included a recipe are self-explanatory and can be found in most standard cookbooks. Others that we deemed too costly, time-consuming, or arcane to reproduce, we listed in the menus solely for your interest. If you care to research the vast and fascinating subject of nineteenth-century cookery further, we direct you to the culinary section of our bibliography. We wish you success with your Victorian-style meals and hearty eating!

ONE

THE VICTORIAN SPIRIT: SETTING THE STAGE

Where we love is home,
Home that our feet may leave, but not our hearts.
—Oliver Wendell Holmes,
Homesick in Heaven, 1872

T HE HOME WAS HELD DEAR IN VICTO-
RIAN HEARTS, AND TO HAVE A HOME
THAT RADIATED CARE AND HAPPINESS
WAS THE VICTORIAN IDEAL. FAMILY
LIFE WAS ONE OF THE BASIC INSTITUTIONS OF VICTO-
RIAN SOCIETY, AND THE CENTER OF FAMILY LIFE WAS
THE HOME. MANY MIDDLE-CLASS VICTORIANS OWNED
THEIR OWN HOMES AND LAVISHED THEIR EXTERIORS
AND INTERIORS WITH DECORATION. TO INVITE
GUESTS—FRIENDS AND FAMILY—INTO ONE'S HOME TO
DRINK AND BREAK BREAD TOGETHER WAS A HIGH COM-
PLIMENT TO THOSE SPECIAL PEOPLE INVITED. EXTEND-
ING AN INVITATION INTO ONE'S DOMESTIC CIRCLE
IMPLIED A HEARTFELT DESIRE TO SHARE ONE'S BOUNTY
WITH OTHERS.

It is this exuberant spirit of generous entertaining that we can hope to emulate in our own homes. Although many aspects of the long and rapidly changing Victorian social era, such as slavery, child labor, and corsets, are best left in the past, for a spirit of welcome, hospitality, and gracious living, we can look to the Victorians to show us the way.

Creating a Victorian-style atmosphere means bringing the era to life. Anyone who has visited a historic home full of period furniture can attest to the beauty of authentic Victorian pieces and restored ornamentation, but often it's the small things one notices—a pair of kid gloves, a fan, a gentleman's top hat, a faded dance card—that give an inkling of the lives of the former inhabitants and make the visit memorable. In fact, the Victorians themselves had a fascination with styles of the past—Gothic, Colonial, Greco-Egyptian—and their homes were often quite eclectic. They accumulated possessions, artifacts, and "keepsakes," cramming tabletops and whatnot shelves with a profusion of objects and mementos. You yourself may collect Victoriana by the shelfload or may just wish to have a Victorian-style ambiance for a special occasion, but distinctive enlivening touches in the Victorian theme can make a visit to your home worth remembering as well. Having the scent of flowers and spices in the parlor or beautiful hanging plants, palms, and ferns—lush, living things and evocative aromas to delight the senses—conveys the Victorian style as much as yards of cretonne or an authentic parlor suite.

PREPARING THE HOUSE
Scented Rooms

Certain aromas and special touches can evoke the timeless Victorian sense of "home" that can make a visitor feel welcome instantly. Your home is your stage for life and whether you have many light and airy rooms or a cozy three- or four-room apartment, it can glow with Victorian hospitality and be redolent with old-fashioned scent.

Though we might think of a Victorian home as stuffy, overheated, or heavily scented, nineteenth-century women appreciated the value of fresh air. As Miss Eliza Leslie suggested to guests in *The Behaviour Book: A Manual for Ladies* (1853):

> *Before you leave the room (bedroom) raise the windows as high as they will go, (unless it should be raining or snowing) that the apartment may be well ventilated. Fortunate are those who have been accustomed to sleeping with the sash more or less open, according to the weather, or the season. Their health will be much the better for the excellent practice of constantly admitting fresh air into their sleeping room. . . . Ladies who follow this practice continue to look young long after those who sleep in close rooms have faded and shrivelled.*

More public rooms such as the parlor or sitting room were certainly aired before visitors entered, opened to allow fresh air to freely circulate and increase the level of oxygen. Rooms for entertaining were clean and orderly, filled with furniture that gleamed with wax and polish, sparkling glassware and mirrors. Though lemon-scented furniture polish might constitute a twentieth-century notion of cleanliness and a sweet-smelling home, Victorian tastes in fragrance ran more toward the redolent blend of spices, herbs, and preserved flowers found in potpourris, pomanders, and stovetop simmers. If you are giving an entertainment in the Victorian style, put your guests in a mood of anticipation with an entryway embellished with touches of Victoriana. A richly painted or stained front door, an elaborate polished door knocker, perhaps a beveled glass lantern and a suggestion of lace at the window—each of these details speaks of a well-cared-for Victorian home. As soon as visitors enter, they can be greeted with the gentle scents of an earlier time wafting from a bowl of potpourri placed on a foyer table.

Another way to add spicy scent to your home is with pomanders. These balls of scent have been known since medieval times, when people wore balls of filigreed silver, gold, or ivory filled with potpourri to ward off disease and to provide a more agreeable personal scent, as bathing was not convenient or common. Today you can find glazed china balls with tiny holes in them designed to be filled with potpourri and hung in a closet or behind the door of a bedroom or bath. The origin of the word *pomme d'ambre* (apple of amber) suggests another type of pomander: apples, oranges, or lemons studded with cloves and cured with spices. A fruit pomander is a simple, old-fashioned way to freshen a closet or linen chest. Heaped in a beautiful bowl, they provide a delightful and fragrant greeting for guests.

An assortment of Victorian accents for today's living, left, includes a fabric-covered picture frame, a sachet rose-patterned band box, an invitation, and a potpourri mixture. Woodland nymphs, above, frolic around the base of this decorative footed vase filled with dried roses.

Pomander Spice Mixture

4 ounces ground cinnamon

2 ounces ground cloves

½ ounce ground allspice

½ ounce ground nutmeg

½ ounce ground mace

1 ounce orrisroot powder

1. Mix all ingredients in a glass or enameled bowl. These amounts are sufficient to cure several pomanders.

2. The mixture can be used over and over. Store in a plastic bag in a dark, cool, dry place.

Makes 8 ounces.

To Make a Pomander

Thin-skinned, firm, sound oranges, lemons, limes, or apples

Whole large-headed, top-quality cloves

Pomander Spice Mixture (recipe above)

Glass, porcelain, or glazed pottery bowl

1. Make holes in fruit skin with a thin skewer and insert cloves, stem end in, into the skin of the fruit. A linear pattern is easier to follow and makes a neat, compact design when finished.

2. If the pomander is to be hung, you can also plan where you want to place your hanging ribbons and leave 4 narrow paths from stem to blossom end of fruit where you do not place cloves. These paths will be where you place the ribbons used to decorate and hang up the pomanders. It is recommended that the studding with the cloves be finished on day started. An unfinished fruit may begin to decay.

3. Spoon half of the pomander spice mixture into large nonmetal bowl and place the studded fruits on top. Sprinkle the rest of the spice mixture over the pomanders.

4. Turn the pomanders every day and sprinkle them anew with the spice mixture.

5. Keep rotating the pomanders and sprinkling them with the spice mixture until the pomanders are completely hardened. Depending on size of fruit this may take anywhere from 2 weeks to a month. When pomanders are hardened they are ready to be decorated with ribbons to be hung up or displayed as desired.

A simple way to dry herbs and flowers, above, is to tie and hang them blossom-end down. Hospitable wreaths can also be made with plant material and hung up to dry. In a floral fantasy, below, we glimpse informal bunches of dried flowers and an imposing arrangement of fresh roses and ivy

A simple way to add old-fashioned fragrance to the home is by concocting stove-top simmers: mixtures of flowers, spices, fruits, herbs, and oils that are combined with water and brought to a simmer on top of the stove. As the steam slowly evaporates, a fragrance is released into the room. Warmth and hospitality are conveyed to guests as the delightful spicy scents of cinnamon and nutmeg waft through the rooms of a home from the kitchen. In fact, the simmer originated to mask pungent cooking odors. Needless to say, the heat must be kept very low so the mixture does not completely evaporate and burn. If, unlike the Victorian kitchen, Cook is not there to keep an eye on the stove while you entertain, you may wish to move the simmer to another room by pouring it into a flameproof container over a candle warmer.

Apple Spice Simmer

1 apple, quartered	1 whole nutmeg, cracked
½ teaspoon whole cloves	¼ vanilla bean
1 cinnamon stick	1 cup water

1. Combine all ingredients in small saucepan, bring to a boil, reduce heat, and allow to simmer uncovered. Watch level of water; if too much evaporates, add more, ½ cup at a time.

2. Or, heat to boiling and pour mixture into a flameproof container over a candle warmer. Add water, if necessary, to keep container about half filled.

Don't underestimate the power of fragrance to create a Victorian mood for your entertainment. Its subtle influence—whether homey and spicy like a simmer, festive and sculptural like a heap of pomanders, or elegant like a potpourri—will set the stage for a delightful "at home."

Using Flowers to Create Atmosphere

Oh roses for the flush of youth
And laurel for the perfect prime;
But pluck an ivy branch for me
Grown old before my time.
—*Christina Rossetti,*
Song, *1862*

Though the preceding sentiment probably doesn't reflect the thoughts of a typical Victorian hostess carefully arranging flowers for the centerpiece for her table, it does give us an inkling of the significance of flowers and plants (particularly roses and ivy) in Victorian daily life. Flowers and plants represented many things to the Victorians; they loved flowers—fresh and dried—and indoor plants, believing that having these expressions of nature in the house fostered a love of beauty and harmony in the soul. Fresh flowers symbolized beauty and youth, dried flowers and grasses were used in funeral bouquets, and an entire "language of flowers" was developed in the

A lush, full-blown arrangement in an iridescent cachepot, left, features peach and pink roses and plumes of heather. Charmingly framed family portraits, above, are clustered on my lady's bureau. Fresh flowers grace the tableau.

mid-nineteenth century to explain hidden messages expressed in the "tussie-mussies," or small bouquets, sent as love tokens. Flower arranging as an art was a particularly Victorian mode of decoration almost exclusively practiced by women. Fortunately, the contemporary host or hostess can indulge in the pleasure of adding fragrance and color to the home without being burdened by Victorian domestic strictures or the fear that guests might get the wrong idea from a particular arrangement of buds and blossoms!

A fresh bouquet certainly adds life and vitality to a room. It conveys the feeling of something living and yet changing and decaying with the passage of time, as well as the sense that caring hands put it where it is to provide beauty and scent. The Victorians commonly placed glass bell jars over fresh arrangements, ostensibly to protect them from the dryness and heat of the drawing-room but unfortunately trapping their fragrance as well. They devoted considerable energy to devising vases and domes that would keep flowers fresh. Dried flower arrangements of roses, geraniums, chrysanthemums, or carnations were also placed under glass dome covers where they would be protected and last for several seasons. In summer months, large arrangements of dried flowers decorated unused fireplaces, which were also sometimes ornamented fancifully with ivy and ferns. Drying flowers was a popular pastime in the 1870s. While you might not have the time or inclination to make elaborate designs with dried flowers pressed and framed as pictures or as glazed panels in doors, as many Victorian ladies did, you can find greeting cards and notepaper with pressed flowers in the Victorian mode. Dried flowers are practical too—the wonderful papery texture and mellow colors of dried hydrangeas or roses can lend an antique air to your living room for months on end.

In a traditional dining room, left, a gilt-framed portrait, striped wallpaper, and dado, along with a splendid chandelier, set the mood. Open lace placemats, tall candlesticks, and flowers make for an inviting setting. Pink roses massed with others and a touch of lace symbolize gentility, below.

If you want a truly authentic Victorian bouquet, fresh or dried, you can't miss with the rose: the "queen of flowers." Roses were the first and most lasting of Victorian flower crazes. In the 1830s and 1840s, numerous new varieties were bred and new species were introduced in Europe and North America. Rosarians point to the development of La France, with its large double flower, by Guillot Fils in 1867 as the beginning of the modern "tea" rose. Rose societies, books on roses, and roses themselves flourished throughout the nineteenth century. Pure yellow roses, sweetly scented miniature roses, immense multiflora roses, were all refined and cherished by the Victorians. We are fortunate indeed that modern hybrid roses are available in colors ranging from pale pastels to the richest reds, but if you're a gardener and can replenish your vases daily, old-fashioned Gallicas and Damasks provide wonderful scent and a less formal arrangement. Reds, pinks, whites, yellows—mass a brilliant bouquet of roses in a packed display as your centerpiece, or make tiny posies in delicate colors for a bathroom vanity.

Actual Victorian arrangements on the dining table were quite elaborate, with an enormous tiered epergne or a tower of fruit and flowers as the focal point. Height was the key, with flowers and ferns in a tall slender vase with fruit (and more ferns) at the base. You may not wish to go to Victorian extremes and have entire living ferns at either end of the table as one hostess did, since visibility could be difficult, but ferns and ivy are important elements in Victorian flower arrangements. Depending on the season and the formality of the occasion consider these displays:

Roses, hydrangea blossoms, anenomes, and baby's breath

Lilacs and tulips in a large basket

Peonies—red, pink, and white

Wild and garden flowers—daisies, clover,
Queen Anne's lace, phlox, daylilies

Bright zinnias alone in a low basket

Long blue delphinium spikes in a decorative cachepot

For historic accuracy in containers, you can use heirloom cut glass vases or Parian porcelain or search out the perfect Art Nouveau piece in an antique shop.

Use flowers to create a Victorian atmosphere throughout the house. A showy bouquet on a table in the hall is a welcoming touch. Or place a lush arrangement of dark rhododendron or laurel leaves in a large vase or cachepot to bring the green outdoors to an entryway. For a less dramatic but equally authentic effect, make small flower arrangements in the tradition of the tussie-mussie. Make posies of herbs, flowers, and foliage or even simple arrangements of violets or pansies or lilies of the valley and place them on a chairside table or bookcase with the Victorian attention to a guest's delight in spotting such a detail.

Suggestions for such diminutive arrangements might be:

Violets alone in a teacup, with saucer

Lilies of the valley in a wine glass

Pink clover and Queen Anne's lace in a brandy snifter

Daisies in a small bowl, placed in a basket

Pansies in an antique creamer

Grape hyacinths in antique glass

A single camellia floating in a silver bowl

Houseplants, too, can create a Victorian ambiance. The Victorian era was the beginning of the houseplant cultivated primarily for indoor decoration, and like everything else they did, the Victorians pursued this interest with gusto, developing elaborate window gardens and glass-walled conservatories. Rare botanical varieties from tropical and subtropical climes were used to compose indoor conservatory landscapes with walls, beds, flowers, and even a garden seat or two for intimate entertaining. Young lovers especially enjoyed the seclusion of the romantic green-leaved conservatory. Ferns and palms were the favored exotics. Their tropical, mysterious, stately foliage fascinated the Victorians; ferns and ivies on marble-topped pedestals and potted palms were placed in the front parlor to be shown off to best advantage.

Flowering exotics were all the rage as well, and many of the fragrant and bright hanging plants that are popular today were cultivated in Victorian greenhouses from specimens brought from Africa, South America, and Asia. The hanging fuchsia from the Orient, with its profusion of vivid blossoms, was a favorite, along with all manner of orchids, the passionflower from South America, the vanilla-scented purple-flowered heliotrope, the jasmine, the unforgettably scented gardenia, and the hibiscus. Common agave begonia, dracaena, caladium, ficus, philodendron, and dieffenbachia were also grown indoors. It is certainly in keeping with the Victorian spirit to create a veritable jungle with any or all of these plants indoors or, in mild climates and in the summertime, outside. For a large home, a potted palm on a stair landing or in a corner of the living room or dining room will give a Victorian effect. Ivies, philodendron, and ferns, along with blossoming plants such as cyclamen, small azaleas, and potted hydrangeas, give a lush impression as well. A showy vivid amaryllis or a choice blossoming orchid on a coffee table can be stunning in a quiet living room. Whether your taste runs to abundance and profusion or dainty and subtle touches, use hothouse plants and flowers to embody the Victorian sensibility in your home.

PREPARING THE PARTY
Splendid Settings

In inviting "a few friends," which means a small select company, endeavor to assort them suitably, so as not to bring together people who have no community of tastes, feelings, and ideas.

—Miss Eliza Leslie,
The Behavior Book: A Manual for Ladies, 1853

The proper blend of guests is an important concern of any host or hostess, whether in the nineteenth century or the late twentieth. In the Victorian era, however, a rigid social order made compiling guest lists a painstaking task. Planning a social event involved complex stratagems, since the proper mix of people at a party was an important means of demonstrating social aspirations. Social climbing was a full-time occupation for those who had made new fortunes in industry and who were anxious to be accepted into Society. Members of each class aspired to move above their present station or at least to the top of their particular heap. The upper classes and those of established wealth made themselves as exclusive as possible.

The most influential American social lioness of the Gilded Age was undisputedly *the* Mrs. Astor. This was Caroline Schermerhorn Astor, wife of William B. Astor, Jr., the playboy grandson of John Jacob, who founded the family fortune.

Mrs. Astor became society's leader using the family fortune, her natural competitiveness, and the cajoling guidance of Ward McAllister. McAllister, a retired lawyer, was a clever, calculating man who drew up a code of manners that would be the last word in deportment of upper-class social life. One may read of his exploits in his memoirs, *Society as I Found It,* from 1890.

❧

The social entertainment that you host will undoubtedly be a more intimate gathering than Mrs. Astor's, more in keeping with the "small select company" which Miss Eliza Leslie describes. Our homes today can capture the elegant hospitality of the Golden Era; splendid settings for Victorian-theme parties are right at hand if we but look imaginatively around us.

A thoughtful touch: placing peonies and baby's breath in a pitcher, above, right. Looking down at a place setting, above.

First decide what kind of event you would like to host. The floor plan of your home or size of your garden will in large part dictate how many people you can accommodate comfortably.

A second consideration, just as it was for your Victorian predecessors, is the season of the year the event is planned for. While you won't be a subject of scandal if you do something "out of season," weather and seasonability can affect the success of your plans. An intimate tea by the fire in chilly autumn or winter seems very appealing. A breezy shaded veranda where refreshing cold drinks can be proffered seems a welcome respite on a sultry afternoon.

Once you've decided on your particular event, factoring in the space you are using and the season of the year, the third consideration (if you're not a Vanderbilt or an Astor) is the amount of money you can allocate to the event. Simplicity has its own form of elegance, so don't bankrupt yourself trying to duplicate an elaborate twenty-course meal! The fourth and final consideration depends on the other three: the number of people you can invite. You may wish to take Miss Eliza Leslie's advice again: "Avoid giving invitations to bores. They will come without."

Victorian-style Invitations

Plan your guest list at least three weeks ahead of your event, checking on addresses and phone numbers. The more formal the event, the earlier the invitations should be sent. This gives added importance to your party. For example, for a formal ball or dinner, send out invitations four weeks ahead. For weddings, four to six weeks ahead of the date is appropriate. For most other social occasions two weeks is ample notice. However, for those friends and acquaintances who travel a great deal, a discreet phone inquiry even before the written invitation is sent, as to whether or not they will be in town on a particular date, is a good idea. But plan on written invitations instead of simple phone calls; they give a sense of formality and anticipation to the receiver and you can convey the Victorian spirit visually with the design and appearance of the invitations.

For your invitations, choose white or pastel cards or notes. The artistic imagination can run full range here. Unique shops that specialize in vintage items stock varied cards, folded blank notes, and printed invitations of Victorian design.

You may choose a simple card bordered with dainty old-fashioned flowers—perhaps roses or pansies. A plain white card with a raised embossed border may be decorated with fine lace ribbon and a simple bow. Pressed dried flowers can be affixed to the card and "tied" with a satin or lace ribbon. Authentic Victorian "scrap" or reproductions of these little paper ornaments can be glued to plain cards to give them a Victorian feel. For Valentine's Day, a red heart placed on a lace doily with cut-out cherubs and a shirred lace border might be your choice. A christening requires the daintiest, most delicate styling, with lace and very narrow pastel blue or pink ribbons.

Invitations for semi-formal or formal (black-tie) dinners and dinner dances can be dramatic. Choose envelopes of a favorite Victorian color: plum, mauve, deep green, burgundy, red, or purple. The invitation itself can be white, written or printed in black ink, tied with narrow satin or velvet ribbons the color of the envelope.

An echo of Victoriana for today is composed of sweet dried blooms, reproduction Victorian valentines, invitations, decorative boxes, and evocative potpourri, above. An eloquently designed silver and crystal tea caddy, opposite page, visually portrays the importance of the contents and the ritual.

On the occasion of a ball, formality and elegance are primary. These invitations can be similar in design to the formal dinner invitation, or to convey the proper sense of grandeur you may wish to have the invitation engraved or printed and embellished with an ornate border in a Victorian mode. The envelope should be white with a liner in a rich jewel tone.

State the exact nature of the function you are inviting the person or persons to, the place and the address, the day of the week, the date, the month, the year, and the time. Indicate how you wish the replies to be received—a phone call, a note, or—for the most formal occasions—filling in a reply card. Indicate proper dress where appropriate: formal or Victorian dress, for example.

As most invitations will be handwritten, except for the larger events, select a fine-point pen, preferably not a ballpoint, to address your invitation in a neat, orderly, and legible handwriting. Consider using the talents of someone who is proficient in a lacy Spencerian script or is an accomplished calligrapher to write the complete invitation, or at the very least the envelope.

When inviting those guests who live within walking or driving distance, a charming Victorian custom is to tie a pretty flower or tiny posy to the invitation with a ribbon and deliver it by hand.

Decorations and Lighting

Once you've put your guests in a mood of anticipation with a charming written invitation and have decided how to create a Victorian-style atmosphere with scent and flowers, plan decorations that complete the effect. You can study photos of period rooms to see the richness and variety of Victorian decor, but it's possible to create a Victorian ambiance without purchasing antique furniture and reproduction wallpaper.

The Victorians loved the pattern and texture of fabrics, especially lace, ribbons, paisley, velvet, and moiré, and they reveled in embellishments of heavy fringes, braid, and tassels. Creating an atmosphere of comfort and warmth was essential and fabric was used to soften every sharp corner. The early Victorian style was characterized by the use of silks and chintzes in light, clear colors and small prints; high Victorian furniture was buttoned, tufted, fringed, shirred, and ruffled and many fabrics had elaborate fruit and flower motifs. The invention of aniline dyes in the 1850s led to the popularity of hot pinks and vibrant violets and blues. These vivid colors can still be found in many Victorian-style paisleys and prints. For a still later look, try reproductions of William Morris prints of intertwining vines in dull greens, rusts, ochers, golds, and peacock blues. Work some of these elements into your rooms: a lace-trimmed cloth placed on a cocktail table, long ribbons and bows tied around doorknobs, a heavy curtain draped in a doorway. A paisley shawl placed on a piano or thrown over a sofa can provide a suitably Victorian ambiance.

If you can find vintage folding fans, long leather opera gloves, a lorgnette, or a lady's beaded silk reticule, compose a nostalgic still life with a dried long-stemmed rose or two added for poignancy. Arrange the objects on a front hall table, the top of a bookcase, or in the master bedroom. Even family portraits displayed on a table in antique frames can create a sense of the era. Highly decorative folding screens can be used to turn a space into a Victorian salon or a Turkish corner. If the screens are too worn, faded, or contemporary in appearance, drape them with a swag of velvet or moiré and tassels to give a period look.

To create the dimmer lighting of the gaslight era, keep the lights in all rooms on the subdued side, changing light bulbs to lower wattages if necessary. For a luscious lighting effect, place spotlights with pink bulbs on the floor to send up a rosy hue. When the lights are placed out of sight below potted palms (rent several from a florist for a special event), the shadows of the exotic greenery create a wonderful mood. And, of course, there's nothing like candlelight and firelight to compliment the complexion and put a sparkle in the eye!

A glimpse of the buffet service shows the Fitz and Floyd "Renaissance" Aubergine service plate, "Montmartre" dinner plate, and "Palladium Fruit" salad plate, above. A stately antique candelabrum adds elegance.

PREPARING THE TABLE
Designing the Table

There were two methods of serving food at table in the last third of the nineteenth century. First was the Old English. In this plan, all the food to be served at each course was placed on the table at once. Each course consisted of several dishes. For example, the first course would include two soups and several fish dishes; the roast course might have roast beef, roast mutton, a roast turkey or goose, and their accompanying sauces and garnishes. The last course combined what the British still call savories and puddings. Mrs. Beeton describes such a last course in *The Book of Household Management* (1861): two ducklings, larded guinea-fowl, orange jelly, charlotte russe, coffee cream, ice pudding, macaroni with Parmesan cheese, and spinach garnished with croutons! All dishes and empty plates were removed at the end of the course, to be replaced by new dishes and plates for the following course, dessert (usually fruit and nuts) being served last.

This elaborate scheme required servants or hired help (or a very nimble host or hostess!) to progress smoothly and often all the food in one course could not be kept hot. Family meals generally had two or three courses and company dinners might have five or more courses.

The second method of serving was "service à la Russe," the Russian style. In this scheme, all the foods to be served were placed on a side table or buffet. Servants, in upper-class homes at least, did the carving and serving. As each course was completed, new dishes of food and fresh plates were placed on the buffet to be served. This method opened up the dining table and opportunity presented itself for elaborate table ornamentation.

The Victorians enthusiastically seized this chance for creativity. To begin with, the plates were set at every place with proper silverware and napkins. For family meals napkins were placed in napkin rings, each person having his own ring so the napkins could be used for subsequent meals. For more formal meals, napkins were frequently folded artistically at each place setting.

The table had one, if not two, floral arrangements. At elaborate dinners, floral and also fruit centerpieces held stage in tall, sometimes tiered, epergnes that rose above the diners' heads. A pair of arrangements might be placed on either side of the epergne or central piece.

When designing a Victorian table today you must consider the meal to be served, time of day, season of the year, and number of people to be served.

Sketch out on a sheet of paper a schema or "floor plan" for your table. If it is a dinner, indicate where the place settings and the floral arrangement or arrangements will be. Will you use candles? Where will they stand? Plan, too, the service table or buffet where you will place foods to be served using the Russian method of service or a combination of English and Russian. Unless you have a serving pantry or a sturdy serving cart, it makes sense to place foods to be served, extra dinner plates, silverware, and cups and saucers on this auxiliary table for convenience.

A Victorian dining room, below, is set for a festive formal dinner. Cherubs hold court with three pedestal vases holding fresh flowers and grapes. Wines are in cut glass decanters at either end of the table.

To cover the table consider using lace or cutwork such as a Battenburg or crocheted cloth. If you do not choose a lace cloth, use a linen cloth and place a lace runner down the center of the table. Lace doilies under floral arrangements or candle holders give an ornate effect. Linens of this sort need not be new. You may be able to find them at tag sales or estate sales. There are many shops—boutiques, really—that specialize in vintage linens, lace, and even clothing.

Next, your napkins. If you're planning a formal sit-down dinner you may want to fold them in a fan or other amusing appropriate shape, or simply tie them with a ribbon and a flower. Another possibility is to use hollow glass napkin rings that can be filled with water to hold little blooms. The bottom of the ring is flat so it can stand erect with the napkin in the ring—a most delightful effect.

Creating Centerpieces

It is important to have height at the table and also varying heights for visual interest. The main, central centerpiece should be the highest element or certainly a very strong focal point. A tiered glass or silver epergne would be ideal, but lacking the appropriate piece, try to be inventive.

A footed cake stand can be placed on the table with another footed stand on top of it secured with florist's tape. Arrange fresh and candied fruits on the pedestal and fill in with shiny green lemon leaves. Ivy is another possibility as it can hang gracefully over the sides. If the table is large, two matching arrangements can be placed equidistant from the center of the table. These twin arrangements can be either fruit or flowers, but keep both the same. Precise arrangements, too, such as topiary trees, can be placed in balanced pairs at either end of a dining room table or set in a progression of three down the center of the table. On a dinner table long strands of ivy can weave gracefully among the candle holders.

The Victorians had a fondness, too, for small individual decorations at each place setting. They might be tiny bouquets arranged in cordial glasses or petite vases or a diminutive rectangular arrangement of flowers repeating the colors of the central arrangement. Accompanying these decorations, but standing apart from them, were place cards with each guest's name written in a spidery script. These place cards were decorated with flowers and embellished borders.

Needless to say we do not advise using all these decorative treatments at one time; choose one or two to grace your table invitingly.

For a tea table, an informal arrangement of old-fashioned flowers would be attractive. Again consider the size and shape of the table. A schema would be helpful here, too. A floral arrangement may be fashioned in a porcelain vegetable dish, a soup tureen, or a cachepot. Baskets are another possibility for centerpieces. Line them with plastic wrap and use florists' "Oasis" to set the flowers into; use florists' tape to crisscross the basket opening to make it more secure. This is an exceptionally pretty treatment for a summer tea, or a spring or summer breakfast.

🌿

The Victorians loved the ritual of the refined consumption of food. Table manners and proper etiquette were important for the well-bred, upwardly mobile person. One of the most visible displays of this preoccupation was the design of countless serving and eating utensils made for very specific uses. Hence the corn cob scrapers, fruit knives and forks, angel cake breakers, cheese scoops, nut and olive picks, bonbon nips, asparagus tongs, piccalilli sets, aspic slicers, mango forks, differently shaped spoons for bouillon cups and soup bowls. Finger bowls, too, were used during this period, brought out before the dessert course.

Some beautiful and esoteric silver eating and serving pieces are still being made today. Some of the richly ornate patterns of the 1870s and 1880s, such as Tiffany's "Audubon" (1871) and "Chrysanthemum" (1880), are still popular with newlyweds. It's also possible to purchase complete sets of lovely old silver in antique shops and at auctions. Of course, your silver should be polished to a fare-thee-well to give all the pieces a cherished, cared-for, old family look.

A service of elaborate desserts, above, beckons from a gleaming Victorian sideboard. A commanding footed centerpiece displaying brilliant flowers, palm fronds, ferns, and fresh fruit, right, cleverly conceals its humble origin: an inverted plastic birdbath!

OUTDOOR OCCASIONS
Porches

The Victorians put their stamp on the out-of-doors, and they loved to entertain there, whether socializing on the veranda or gathering in the garden's gazebo. Houses with turrets and balustrades, crockets and finials, often had well-groomed lawns and gardens suitable for tea and cucumber sandwiches with the vicar's wife or gentle games of croquet or lawn tennis.

Victorian houses designed in the carpenter gothic, stick, and Queen Anne styles—or combinations of all three—frequently had the benefit of generous verandas. These open-air or partially closed porches might simply apron the front of a home, sweep around on two sides, or even take command of the dwelling on both levels as in the "steamboat gothic" style.

Such a pleasing area to sit in, partly in open view to passersby and partly hidden, enjoying welcome shade and cool breezes, the Victorian porch was the scene of many social events.

Wicker furniture painted white or green or left its natural color reigned on the Victorian porch. There, one could find armchairs, love seats, chaise longues, rockers, and end tables all fashioned of wicker with varying degrees of ornamentation. Plump cushions covered with floral fabric made the seating comfortable.

The porch floor was painted to complement the coloring of the house—frequently the porch ceiling was painted pale blue to emulate the sky. Rush matting from the Orient covered the floor of the porch, and sometimes even an Oriental carpet was placed here and there on the floor if the home was grand and the porch large.

Hanging plants such as fuchsia, geranium, and ivies in rustic work, or twig, baskets or on French bronzed brackets added color and greenery to the porch. Green plants on wicker stands added decoration, too. In the summer a house party could be enlivened with paper lanterns strung up on the porch and glass or bamboo wind chimes placed where the faintest breeze could make them tinkle.

The gracious porch was a welcome respite from the inside of a stuffy home in those days before air conditioning. We too can use our porches or patios in much the same manner. White or natural wicker furniture, soft floral cushions, candles placed in sturdy glass hurricane lamps, rush matting, and even a few old Oriental throw rugs can all add romantic comfort.

Window boxes can be built to hang at the porch rails and planted with flowers. Hanging plants—ferns and ivies and those that bloom—are delightful. You might want to install one or two big-bladed electric ceiling fans to move the air and also add their own level of nostalgia.

Gardens

The garden was chosen for many summer entertainments by the Victorians. Grassy rolling lawns edged by lush blooming flower beds were natural settings for social occasions.

We know that Victorians loved flowers and exotic plants. Their love of decoration and

ornamentation was expressed in the garden as well—a garden path leading through an arched trellis covered in rambling roses might lead to a grassy dell. In the center of the green a sundial might be placed on a sturdy pedestal, surrounded by heavy, white-painted, filigreed cast-iron garden furniture—a love seat for two was popular. Another choice might be the cast-iron furniture made to look like gnarled tree branches or rustic "twig" furniture.

Statuary, perhaps a cherub or animal such as a deer, might be placed in a semi-hidden bower to be discovered on a walk through the garden.

On rolling lawns, the Victorians enjoyed croquet, an approved outdoor activity for men and women to participate in together. Badminton and lawn tennis were played on the lawns of grand homes. Here, too, women could play with men as their partners. Blind Man's Bluff was another lawn game, albeit fairly unstructured, an amusing Victorian ice breaker.

All these outdoor activities demanded refreshments. Cakes, sweetmeats, cool drinks, and ices were offered and enjoyed on stone terraces or under trellised grapevines.

Cast-iron furniture set out on a sunny lawn, left, awaits the guests. A cast-iron urn planted with geraniums, above, graces a Victorian porch. In Saratoga Springs, New York, right, an open porch displays a lace-covered table offering Banana Apricot Cake, tea sandwiches, Pâte à Choux Puffs with Curried Chicken Salad, and Old-Fashioned Lemonade.

TWO

VICTORIAN MORNINGS

*I*N THE VICTORIAN ERA THE INDUSTRIOUS BUSINESSMEN—AND THEIR WIVES—OF THE MIDDLE CLASS BEGAN TO SUPPLANT THE LEISURED NOBILITY AND GENTRY AS THE DOMINANT INFLUENCE ON SOCIAL CUSTOMS. SUBURBAN LIVING AND THE DAILY COMMUTE BEGAN TO BE PART OF THE DAILY ROUTINE. MORNINGS WERE BUSTLING, BUSY, AND ENERGETIC. THERE WAS WORK TO BE DONE, AND THE WHOLE FAMILY ROSE EARLY AND HAD A SUBSTANTIAL MEAL TO ENABLE THEM TO BEGIN THE DAY'S ACTIVITIES WITH VIGOR. IN A LARGE, AFFLUENT HOUSEHOLD, ONE OR MORE SERVANTS WOULD ROUSE THEMSELVES VERY EARLY TO PREPARE THE BREAKFAST TABLE. IN MORE MODEST HOMES THE LADY OF THE HOUSE WOULD CHOOSE AND COOK THE MEAL.

Substantial is, perhaps, an understatement: well-to-do Victorians continued to eat breakfasts more suited to their farming or fox-hunting ancestors. Mrs. Beeton suggests cold roasts, game, or poultry; veal-and-ham or game-and-steak pies; broiled mackerel, whiting, herring, and dried haddock; steak, mutton chops, and kidneys; along with eggs, bacon, ham, sausage, porridge, and toast. In America, baked beans and fish balls might supplant the meat pies; muffins, waffles, and pancakes supplement the toast ("muffins" in England are different, and were more common at tea than at breakfast); and in the South hominy grits might take the place of porridge. Toward the end of the nineteenth century, however, an American author, M. E. W. Sherwood, in her *Art of Entertaining* (1892), shows an awareness that not everyone wanted such a gargantuan meal that early. "The appetite is in a parlous state at nine o'clock and needs to be tempted," she wrote, and advised that "a slice of fresh melon, a plate of strawberries, . . . bread and butter may be much better for breakfast in summer than the baked beans and stewed codfish of a later season."

In the country houses of the leisured classes in both England and America, this mammoth breakfast might be set out, buffet style, for household members and guests to help themselves at whatever time they liked. Such a service was a holdover from the previous era: Lady Caroline Lamb (Lord Byron's inamorata) wrote in 1805 of staying at a country house where breakfast was served from daybreak till dinner.

In middle-class homes, or in the cities, breakfast would be eaten by the family at an early hour, after which the husband would depart for work, the children for school (if they were not away at boarding school), much as today. Still, the meal was not rushed as our modern-day breakfasts so often are, and as we have seen it was much more than our juice, coffee, and rolls. But just as our ideal morning meal is held in a sunny breakfast nook, so the Victorian breakfast took place, if possible, in a room that caught the early rays of the sun, at a table decorated with fresh flowers or a pot of ivy. Many large English houses had a separate "breakfast parlour" for serving this meal, rather than using the large and stately formal dining room.

After breakfast, the middle-class Victorian lady of the house was expected to deal with domestic concerns. This might involve no more than issuing a few directions to a competent housekeeper, or she might have to do a fair amount of the chores herself, possibly with the assistance of a daily maid-of-all-work.

However, as leisure and creativity permitted, special morning social events might be planned. Some of these, along with the traditional breakfast, lend themselves to re-creation on a weekend or holiday morning, as a gracious beginning to the day. If you are fortunate enough to have a formal dining room with a sideboard, the formidable, highly sustaining English Breakfast with its wide choice of appetizing dishes is an elegant morning repast. The less formal Berry Breakfast is a natural for the summertime, exploiting the delights of seasonal fresh garden berries. Another pleasant choice is the Cozy Morning Tea.

A tea table, below, shows lace cloth placed over a handsome quilted cloth, decorative tea service pieces, cookies on a little tea rack, and grapes in a basket with ivy entwined around the handles.

ENGLISH BREAKFAST

Now to the banquet we press;
Now for the eggs, the ham;
Now for the mustard and cress;
Now for the strawberry jam.

Now for the tea of our host,
Now for the rollicking bun;
Now for the muffins and toast. . .

—*W. S. Gilbert,*
The Sorcerer, 1877

In large, wealthy Victorian households that maintained servants, members of the family and visiting guests helped themselves to breakfast dishes that had been previously prepared and placed on the dining room sideboard rather than being served each dish. This mode of eating the English breakfast arose because the servants ate their breakfast in the kitchen at the same time as the whole family did.

On a massive, ornately carved, often mirrored, and sometimes marble-topped sideboard, a varied selection of hearty foods was presented. Each family member except the very littlest, after choosing his or her own food, would sit down at the previously set dining room table to eat.

For the prosperous, securely situated Victorian family the ritual of breakfasting together and enjoying a substantial meal sustained their unspoken belief that they were empire builders. And empire builders did not get up late to start the day with simple tea, coffee, and rolls.

The sideboard is laden with food: a cut-glass compote with plump stewed prunes, orange slices, and cinnamon sticks; a chafing dish of hickory-smoked ham, country sausages, and mushrooms; and platters of sunny-side-up fried eggs with a sprinkling of fresh herbs, crisply grilled marinated quail, and baked stuffed tomatoes. A covered tureen might reveal oatmeal porridge to be served with thick cream and sugar. Assorted hot rolls and hearty breads were put out along with butter and Seville orange marmalade. A final dish was a generous bowl of fresh fruits. Coffee, tea, and hot chocolate were the beverages of choice.

❧

While certainly not a meal for every day, you might like to serve this repast or a similar one on a long weekend—perhaps in fall or winter when morning appetites need rousing.

The menu lends itself to buffet presentation and you can follow the Victorian example. You may not have an elaborate sideboard—use it by all means if you do—but you can use your dining room table effectively to arrange the fruit bowl, serving dishes, and hot and cold foods. A smaller side table can be used for plates, silverware, and cups and saucers if need be.

A polished bare wood table might be a suitable choice. Place a lace runner down the center and use individual doilies under platters as the Victorians would have done. Center this table with a bountiful arrangement of fresh fruits—to be selected and eaten if desired.

Stewed Prunes with Orange Slices and Cinnamon Sticks in a silver compote, above, are a fitting way to begin a traditional English breakfast.

MENU

ENGLISH BREAKFAST

Stewed Prunes with Orange Slices and Cinnamon Sticks*

Sautéed Hickory-smoked Ham, Sausages, and Mushrooms*

Fried Eggs with Fresh Herbs

Grilled Marinated Quail*

Baked Stuffed Tomatoes*

Oatmeal Porridge   Milk   Vanilla Sugar   Brown Sugar

Hearty Seven-grain Bread   Butter   Seville Orange Marmalade

Bowl of Fresh Fruits in Season:
Oranges, Peaches, Plums, Grapes, Apples, Bananas

Coffee   Tea   Herbal Teas   Hot Chocolate

*Recipe given

Stewed Prunes with Orange Slices and Cinnamon Sticks

Stewed prunes had origins in Victorian England. It took just a little imagination to pair them with oranges and scent them with cinnamon and vanilla.

1 12-ounce package pitted prunes	2 cinnamon sticks
1 vanilla bean, halved	1 medium-sized navel orange

1. Place 3 cups water, prunes, vanilla bean, and cinnamon sticks in 3-quart saucepan.

2. Slice unpeeled orange crosswise into ¼-inch slices. Add to prunes.

3. Place over medium-high heat, bring to a boil, reduce heat, and boil gently 5 minutes. Remove from heat and cool.

4. Store in covered glass jar in refrigerator. Will keep up to 3 weeks.

Makes 1 quart.

Sautéed Hickory-smoked Ham, Sausages, and Mushrooms

Meats, especially smoked meats, were required for a truly hearty Victorian breakfast table. We offer an appetizing combination of smoked ham and sausages along with mushrooms, which were also a Victorian favorite.

3 tablespoons butter	¼ cup chicken broth
1 8-ounce slice smoked center-cut ham	¼ teaspoon dried or ½ teaspoon
1 pound sausages (use large, sometimes	fresh thyme
called "dinner," sausages)	½ teaspoon dried or 1 tablespoon
1 pound mushrooms	chopped fresh sage
	3 sage sprigs for garnish

1. In large skillet heat 2 tablespoons butter until hot but not smoking. Add ham slice and brown on both sides. Remove to plate and set aside.

2. In same skillet place sausages and 3 tablespoons water; cover and cook over low heat 5 minutes, shaking pan frequently.

3. Remove cover from pan, increase heat, and brown sausages, turning to brown both sides. When brown remove to plate with ham slice.

4. Wipe mushrooms clean with a damp paper towel. Cut off stems if large and slice crosswise; leave caps whole.

5. Add remaining butter to skillet and melt. Add mushroom caps and sliced stems. Cook over medium heat for 3 minutes, stirring frequently.

6. Add ham steak, sausages, broth, thyme, and sage to pan. Cover and cook

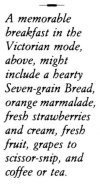

A memorable breakfast in the Victorian mode, above, might include a hearty Seven-grain Bread, orange marmalade, fresh strawberries and cream, fresh fruit, grapes to scissor-snip, and coffee or tea.

until heated through, about 5 minutes.

7. Cut ham steak crosswise into 2-inch-wide strips. Place ham strips, sausages, mushrooms, and pan drippings in chafing dish to serve. Garnish with fresh sage sprigs.

Makes 6 servings.

Grilled Marinated Quail

Wild birds of all kinds were plentiful during Victorian times. Quail, part of the game scene, were enjoyed in varied preparations. This recipe for Grilled Marinated Quail might well serve as an unusual first course at a dinner.

6 quail

1 cup white wine or ½ cup white wine
 and ½ cup tarragon vinegar

¼ cup olive oil

1 teaspoon dried sage or thyme

1 small onion, quartered

3 cloves

½ teaspoon salt, or to taste

½ teaspoon freshly ground black
 pepper

6 slices white or cracked wheat
 bread

2 tablespoons butter

Parsley sprigs for garnish

Currant or crab apple jelly

1. Split the quail, spreading open but not cutting apart.

2. In a shallow, non-corrodible dish, such as a glass pie pan or baking pan, combine wine or wine/vinegar mixture, olive oil, sage, onion, and cloves. Mix well.

3. Place the quail in the marinade, turning to coat both sides. Cover with plastic wrap and refrigerate a few hours or overnight.

4. Arrange the quail on a rack in a shallow baking pan. Brush with some of the marinade and sprinkle with salt and pepper.

5. Roast at 450° for 20 minutes, basting well with marinade once during that time. Or place quail under broiler 4 inches from heat source and broil about 8 to 10 minutes per side, seasoning with salt and pepper and basting with marinade.

6. Toast bread, butter, and cut each slice in half, making two triangles. Arrange on serving plate, placing quail on toast triangles. Garnish with parsley. Serve with currant or crab apple jelly.

Makes 6 breakfast servings or 3 dinner servings.

Baked Stuffed Tomatoes

Mrs. Beeton's *English Cookery* describes three different preparations for stuffed tomatoes. The recipe given is a straightforward variation that owes its flavor to the herb-seasoned bread stuffing.

6 medium-sized tomatoes

⅓ cup butter

¼ cup finely chopped green onion or onion

2 tablespoons finely chopped parsley

½ teaspoon dried or 1½ teaspoons chopped fresh tarragon

½ teaspoon dried or 1½ teaspoons chopped fresh rosemary

¼ teaspoon salt, or to taste

¼ teaspoon freshly ground black pepper

2 cups small (⅜-inch) bread cubes (use a firm white bread)

1. Preheat oven to 375°.

2. Cut ½-inch slice from stem end of each tomato. With teaspoon, scoop out a hollow about 1 inch deep in each tomato. Cut a thin slice from blossom end if necessary so tomato will sit upright.

3. Heat butter in skillet and sauté green onion or onion, parsley, tarragon, and rosemary 1 to 2 minutes. Add salt, pepper, and bread squares. Mix well with a fork.

4. Lightly fill tomatoes with stuffing, piling high in center.

5. Bake in a shallow glass baking pan for 20 to 25 minutes or until browned. Makes 6 servings.

An impressive baked ham such as this mustard-glazed ham garnished with parsley and grapes, right, might be the star at an elaborate English Breakfast accompanying Stewed Prunes with Orange Slices and Cinnamon Sticks, as served at The Mansion in Rock City Falls, New York.

BERRY BREAKFAST

'Long about knee-deep in June,
'Bout the time strawberries melts
On the vine.

—James Whitcomb Riley,
<u>Knee-Deep in June,</u> 1883

It might even be the middle of July or yet toward mid-August when a full range of wild and cultivated berries were available in the patches and markets of the nineteenth century. Mrs. Beeton gives the following schedule for when berries were ripe and available in England:

MAY gooseberries • strawberries

JUNE gooseberries • raspberries • strawberries

JULY gooseberries • raspberries • strawberries • currants

AUGUST gooseberries • raspberries • mulberries • currants

SEPTEMBER mulberries

The Victorians loved these colorful jewel-like fruits and spent many outings picking berries in the sunny fields and the dappled thickets where they grew.

A Berry Breakfast with all the available berries (strawberries, gooseberries, blackberries, blueberries, raspberries) assembled and served in a myriad of ways was a poetic tribute to their fleeting presence. Today, we can get the commoner raspberries, blueberries, and strawberries year-round, though the traveled, refrigerated, modern berry can't compare with the taste of the fresh, succulent varieties, wild and cultivated, available, if only seasonally, to the Victorians. Have your Berry Breakfast in the summer when the best native berries are available. If possible, organize a picking expedition to provide your own provender as the Victorians did.

The front porch or a garden bower is an appropriate airy, green location for the Berry Breakfast. Start with a white linen, deep-fringed cloth and napkins. Use pressed- or cut-glass bowls, hand-painted flower- and fruit-patterned china bowls, plates, cups, and saucers. Berries and other fruits were themes that Victorian ladies painted on china as a pastime. Assemble pitchers of various sizes for cream, milk, honey, and syrup. Use ornate Victorian silver berry spoons, special spoons called sugar shells, and cake servers. For individual silverware, use your most elaborate patterns.

The Berry Breakfast can be a small buffet or set up on a table where everything to be served is placed on the table at once. Coffee, tea, and herb teas can be poured at request.

A Victorian Berry Breakfast seems an excellent way to begin a leisurely summer Sunday or to invigorate a trim white-clad group before a set of mixed doubles. Or serve it at a mid-morning ladies' fashion show.

MENU

BERRY BREAKFAST

Bowls of Fresh Berries: Blackberries, Blueberries, Raspberries, Strawberries

Fresh Thick Cream　　Crème Fraîche　　Sour Cream　　Yogurt

Sugar　　Confectioners' Sugar　　Dark Brown Sugar　　Colored Sugar Crystals

Minted Honey

Cinnamon Toast Fingers　　Popovers*

Buttermilk Pancakes　　Raspberry Syrup　　Grilled Country Sausage Links

Blueberry Muffins* or Blueberry Buckle*

Strawberry Butter*

Coffee　　Tea　　Herbal Teas

* Recipe given

Popovers

Popovers get their name from their characteristic ballooning over the tops of the baking cups, which results from the steam leavening.

3 eggs   1 cup sifted all-purpose flour

1 cup milk   ½ teaspoon salt

3 tablespoons vegetable oil

1. Preheat oven to 400°. Grease cast-iron popover pan or eight 5-ounce custard cups.

2. In bowl beat eggs, milk, and oil until well combined.

3. Sift flour with salt over egg mixture; beat just until smooth.

4. Pour batter into prepared popover pan or custard cups, filling each half full. If using custard cups, place them on a baking sheet.

5. Bake 40 to 45 minutes until deep golden brown and puffed. Serve hot.

Makes 8 popovers.

The Inn at Fernbrook, Massachusetts, on Cape Cod, right, provides the perfect setting for a Berry Breakfast on the wicker-furnished porch. Strawberry-Cranberry Slush in glasses, warm Blueberry Muffins, butter, honey, a cut glass bowl of berries, sugar, cream, and hot coffee make a delightful meal.

Blueberry Muffins

There's something warm and comforting about muffins; as for Blueberry Muffins, why, they're just the best—telling of summer and sunshine.

2 cups all-purpose flour

½ cup sugar

1 tablespoon baking powder

½ teaspoon salt

1 cup blueberries

1 cup milk

⅓ cup vegetable oil or melted

    vegetable shortening

1 egg, lightly beaten

Sugar

1. Preheat oven to 400°. Grease one 12-cup or two 6-cup muffin pans.

2. In large bowl, combine flour with sugar, baking powder, and salt. Stir in blueberries.

3. Combine milk, oil, and egg; beat with fork to mix.

4. Make a well in center of flour-blueberry mixture. Pour in milk mixture all at once. Stir quickly with fork, just until dry ingredients are moistened; do not over mix. Batter will be lumpy.

5. Using a rounded ¼-cup measure, spoon batter into muffin pan cups. Sprinkle tops lightly with sugar.

6. Bake 20 to 25 minutes or until golden and cake tester inserted in center comes out clean.

7. Let cool 3 minutes; loosen muffins carefully with spatula and turn out. Serve hot with butter.

Makes 12 large muffins.

A lacy napkin lines a basket of Blueberry Muffins, and a bowl holds honey to drizzle over fresh berries, above.

A summer morning in the garden at Grace Place Bed and Breakfast, Greenwood, South Carolina, right, brings a honeydew melon cut in the shape of a swan and filled with fruit. Other offerings include blueberries, cantaloupe, waffles with whipped cream, blueberries and strawberries, and iced tea.

Blueberry Buckle

Blueberry Buckle: this whimsical name for a quick coffee cake no doubt originated from the bucket one often buckled to one's belt while picking blueberries.

CAKE

¾ cup sugar	½ teaspoon ground nutmeg
¼ cup butter, softened	½ teaspoon ground cinnamon
2 eggs	2 cups blueberries
½ cup milk	
1½ cups all-purpose flour	TOPPING
2 teaspoons baking powder	½ cup sugar
¼ teaspoon ground cloves	⅓ cup all-purpose flour
	½ teaspoon ground cinnamon
	¼ cup butter, softened

1. Preheat oven to 375°. Grease a 9-inch square cake pan.

2. In large bowl beat together sugar and butter with electric mixer. Add eggs and milk and beat until well blended.

3. Stir in flour, baking powder, cloves, nutmeg, and cinnamon. Mix at low speed until blended. Fold in blueberries.

4. Clean side of bowl and beaters. Turn batter into prepared pan and spread evenly.

5. For topping, mix sugar, flour, cinnamon, and butter with pastry blender or two knives until crumbly. Sprinkle evenly over top of batter.

6. Bake 45 minutes or until cake tests done. Serve warm, cut into squares.

Makes 9 to 12 squares.

Strawberry Butter

Strawberry Butter, a great way to use very ripe berries, is perfect for muffins, toast, scones, and popovers.

½ cup butter, softened	1 tablespoon confectioners' sugar
¼ cup chopped ripe strawberries	

1. Combine butter, strawberries, and confectioners' sugar in blender or food processor and blend until combined. Pack into crock or small ramekin, cover surface with plastic wrap or foil, and refrigerate until needed.

Makes ½ cup.

COZY MORNING TEA

The cosy fire is bright and gay,
The merry kettle boils away
And hums a cheerful song.
I sing the saucer and the cup:
Pray, Mary, fill the teapot up,
And do not make it strong.
—Barry Pain,
The Poets at Tea: "Cowper"

By the Victorian era, formal calls, though still termed "morning calls" (in the eighteenth and early nineteenth centuries they had been made in the morning), were an afternoon ritual. But in between the morning domestic chores and the afternoon social chores, a lady might have time for a cozy chat with a real friend or two. In a conservatory or gazebo in the summer, or before the parlor fire in winter, over tea and light and elegant tidbits, good friends would share gossip, secrets, and household and sewing hints in a relaxed, comfortable setting.

Another occasion for socializing was the working party: a group of ladies would meet to sew their own clothes or clothes for the poor, or to embroider church linens. Sometimes one woman would read aloud while the rest plied their needles. Then, at the end, there would be time for "the cup that cheers but not inebriates."

In either case, the tea, of course, would be "real" loose tea—not what one British wit called "those little laundry bags"—served from a pot. Old tea services have two pots, a small one for the tea essence and a larger one for hot water; individual cups could thus be mixed to the desired strength. Miss Eliza Leslie advises in *The Behaviour Book: A Manual for Ladies* (1853): "In pouring out, do not fill the cups to the brim. Always send the cream and sugar round, that each person may use those articles according to their own taste." The sugar would be lump sugar ("One lump or two?"). At one time it was considered bad form to use plates at a tea party, so any goodies served with the tea would have to be capable of being consumed in one neat and dainty bite. In England, plates were acceptable, but the shibboleth was never to bite anything in two: toast or bread, muffins or cake would be broken into bite-sized bits to be taken whole into the mouth.

☘

We can recapture the charms of such a tea party today, inviting a special friend or two on a lazy vacation morning or an unstructured weekend one. Set your table with a cloth and napkins— cotton or linen, simple or decorative, but always freshly laundered and spotless. If you have a silver tea service, polish it up (the British use a simple mixture of whiting and ammonia, and elbow grease); if not, use your prettiest china pot and daintiest cups and saucers. Use real tea, and serve some homemade dainties to go with it.

COZY MORNING TEA

Earl Grey Tea   Orange Clove Tea   Vanilla Milk Tea
Lemon Slices   Milk   Cream

Cinnamon Spiral Raisin Bread*   Currant Scones*

Fresh Dairy Cottage Cheese with Fresh Fruit

Orange Butter*   Blueberry Jam   Fig Preserves

*Recipe given

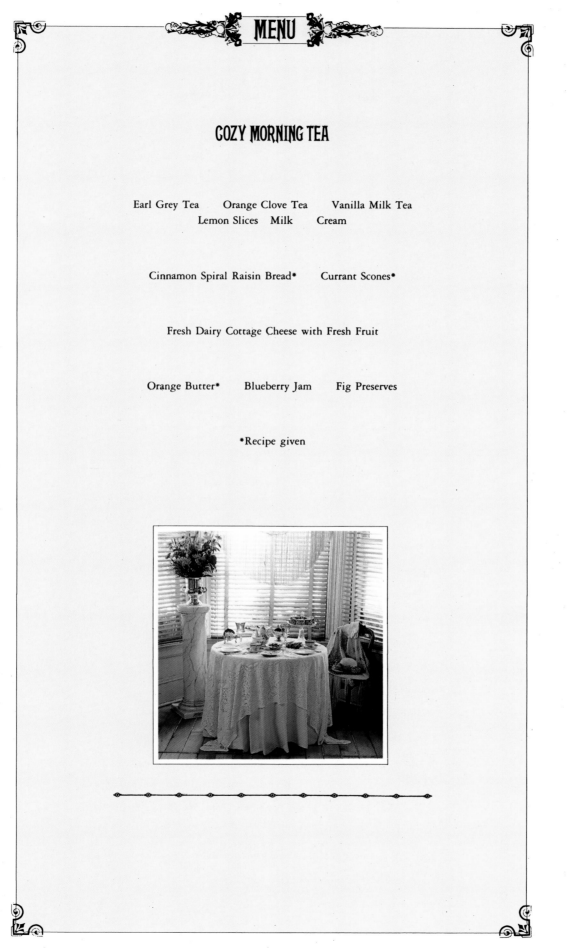

Cinnamon Spiral Raisin Bread

What better way for a Victorian cook to display her baking skills than by baking a plump brown loaf of Cinnamon Spiral Raisin Bread? Wonderful freshly baked and great toasted, this bread's raisins seem to promote freshness.

2 cups raisins	4 tablespoons butter, softened
½ cup apple juice	2 eggs
1 package active dry yeast or yeast cake	5 to 6 cups all-purpose flour
	4 tablespoons butter, softened
1 teaspoon sugar	4 teaspoons ground cinnamon
¼ cup very warm water	½ cup sugar
1¾ cups milk	1 egg yolk
⅓ cup sugar	¼ cup cream
1 tablespoon salt	

1. Place raisins in small bowl, pour apple juice over them, and cover. Let stand overnight to plump. Drain.

2. Dissolve yeast and 1 teaspoon sugar in warm water. Heat milk in saucepan until a ring of bubbles forms around side of pan. Cool until warm.

3. In a large bowl combine warm milk, ⅓ cup sugar, salt, and 4 tablespoons butter. Add yeast mixture and eggs. Gradually beat in 3 cups flour. Beat well.

4. Using a heavy wooden spoon, gradually stir in enough additional flour to make a stiff dough. Stir in 1 cup of the raisins.

5. Turn dough out on floured surface and knead until smooth, elastic, and glossy, about 10 minutes.

6. Place dough in a large (3-quart) buttered bowl and turn well so the entire surface is lightly coated with butter.

7. Cover and allow to rise until doubled in bulk, about 2½ hours.

8. Grease well two 9 × 5 × 3-inch loaf pans.

9. Punch dough down with fist. Knead again, about 6 to 8 minutes.

10. Divide the dough into two parts and roll each into a rectangle about 20 × 7 inches.

11. Spread each rectangle with 2 tablespoons soft butter. Sprinkle remaining 1 cup raisins over each buttered rectangle, dividing equally. Mix cinnamon and sugar together and sprinkle over raisins.

12. Roll each rectangle tightly, starting from the short side, and place in pans. Cover and let rise in a warm place until loaves completely fill pans and extend above the tops. Preheat oven to 400°.

Clove-studded lemon slices, opposite page, above, are arranged in an overlapping spiral ready for tea. On a lace-covered table, opposite page, below, slices of Cinnamon Spiral Raisin Bread, butter curls, sugar, and a teapot are ready for an informal morning tea.

13. Brush tops with mixture of 1 egg yolk and ¼ cup cream. Bake at 400° for 20 minutes, then reduce heat to 350°. Continue baking an additional 20 to 30 minutes or until loaves sound hollow when rapped with knuckles or a wooden spoon. Turn out of pans and cool on rack.

Makes 2 loaves.

Orange Butter

The Victorians thriftily used all parts of the orange for this tasty complement to biscuits, toast, or scones.

1 tablespoon finely grated orange zest	2 teaspoons honey
½ cup butter, softened	2 tablespoons orange juice

1. In bowl using electric mixer or in bowl of food processor using metal chopping blade, combine orange zest, butter, honey, and orange juice.

2. Beat or process to blend thoroughly. Pack into 6- to 8-ounce crock. Serve immediately or cover and refrigerate until ready to serve.

Makes ¾ cup.

Currant Scones

Scones—the beloved quick bread (quick because it is made with baking powder and not yeast and therefore requires no rising time)—originate from England. They're a favorite at tea time, especially "elevenses," the late morning ritual scheduled to refresh the spirit and succor the appetite.

SCONES

2 cups all-purpose flour	¼ cup vegetable shortening
2½ teaspoons baking powder	½ cup dried currants
2 tablespoons sugar	1 egg
1 teaspoon salt	½ cup milk

TOPPING

2 tablespoons milk or cream	1 tablespoon sugar

1. Preheat oven to 450°.

2. In a mixing bowl combine flour, baking powder, sugar, and salt. Mix lightly.

3. Add shortening to the flour mixture and cut in, using a pastry blender or two knives, until mixture is crumbly. Stir in currants.

4. Add egg to milk and beat with a fork. Pour egg and milk into the flour mixture, mixing only until dry ingredients are moistened. Using a rubber scraper and your hands, make a ball of the dough, pressing until it holds together.

5. Dust wooden counter or pastry board with flour. Place dough on surface and knead ten times. Lightly press dough into a circle about 8 inches in diameter and about ¾-inch thick.

6. Brush top of dough with milk or cream and sprinkle with sugar. Cut into six pie-shaped wedges for large scones, twelve for regular-sized scones. Place scones 1 inch apart on ungreased baking sheet and bake 10 to 12 minutes for regular scones and 12 to 15 minutes for large scones, or until tops are golden brown. Serve hot, with butter and jam as desired.

Makes 6 large scones or 12 regular scones.

Crusty, tender Currant Scones, above, are arranged on a glass pedestal ready to be served with butter, jam, or marmalade, and accompanied by a cup of tea.

MORNING BRUNCH

Though the term "brunch" is of fairly recent origin, the meal it denotes has been around for a long time. The *Oxford English Dictionary* traces the term to university slang of the last years of the nineteenth century. But fashionable people who danced into the wee hours of the morning—which they have been doing since at least the eighteenth century—would rise late and not take their breakfast until nearly noon, or even later. There were also the late morning or early afternoon meals taken in company and called "breakfasts"—the hunt club breakfast or the literary and scientific breakfasts of learned Londoners and Bostonians, such as the Saturday Club, are examples. These meals were much what we would now call brunch. A Boston "breakfast" given in honor of Oliver Wendell Holmes included clams, grilled trout, mushroom omelet, plover, filet mignon, and asparagus hollandaise, along with potatoes, salad, and dessert.

Then there was the Continental *déjeuner à la fourchette.* English or American visitors touring the Continent or stopping at fashionable watering places must have been shocked to be offered nothing but coffee and a roll or bread for breakfast, and must have been only too ready to tuck into the noon meal. In French, both breakfast and the noon meal are called *déjeuner*—the morning roll and coffee is *petit déjeuner,* the more substantial midday meal, *déjeuner à la fourchette* or "fork breakfast." Substantial luncheons called by the French name *déjeuner à la fourchette* became very popular with fashionable New Yorkers about the 1840s or 1850s.

On an ornately-carved Victorian sideboard, left, the components of a Morning Brunch are arranged from left to right: Huntington Carrots, Butter-braised Chicken with Garden Herbs, and Celery Victor St. Francis.

On the antique oak sideboard, right, drinks are offered: Pisco Punch with pineapple sticks, Raspberry Shrub with raspberries, and a decanter filled with brandy.

Whatever it was called, we can picture a convivial company of splendidly attired Victorians enjoying such a meal to revive their spirits and spark their energy. Possibly they are sitting in a dining room with grand French doors leading out to a gallery or porch hung with baskets of blooming flowers.

※

To reprise such an occasion, plan a fresh yet tranquil color scheme such as butter yellow, green, and peach, or peach, green, and white. Fill baskets or vases with large blooms: hydrangeas, peonies, daylilies. Palms and ferns can add their mood-evoking charm. Pick up the foundation color of butter yellow or peach in your table linens, have your china and serving dishes in cream or white, and add green accents with ribbons or accessories. Mass a tall arrangement of pale yellow and peach flowers and green leaves in the center of the table, with a smaller arrangement at each side. Wrap satin ribbon around the base of the containers.

The menu for this party is American, fairly sophisticated, and hearty: the Pisco Punch, Celery Victor St. Francis, and Angels on Horseback supply a San Francisco flavor.

MENU

MORNING BRUNCH

Pisco Punch*   Red Raspberry Shrub*

Angels on Horseback*

Celery   Radishes   Olives   Carrots

Corned Beef Hash   Poached Eggs

Butter-braised Chicken with Garden Herbs*

Celery Victor St. Francis*

Creamed Huntington Carrots

Avocado Halves with Louis Dressing

Pickled Peaches

Cinnamon Raisin Sticky Buns

Sourdough Bread

Butter

Coffee   Tea

*Recipe given

Pisco Punch

This potent punch combines brandy, grape juice, and pineapple juice with a hint of anise-flavored liqueur.

½ ounce Pernod

2 ounces Pisco Peruvian or other brandy

1 ounce white grape juice

Crushed ice

6 ounces chilled pineapple juice

Pineapple sticks or chunks for garnish

1. Coat the inside of a tall glass with Pernod by swirling the liqueur around the glass. Discard any of the liqueur that does not adhere.

2. Pour brandy into the glass and add grape juice. Fill glass with crushed ice.

3. Pour chilled pineapple juice over all, filling glass to the brim. Garnish with pineapple stick.

Makes 1 serving.

Red Raspberry Shrub

Plentiful berries are the base for tempting—sometimes devastating—drinks. Shrubs are made with fruit and brandy or rum and were commonly served in colonial America.

2 cups fresh red raspberries or 1 10-ounce package frozen red raspberries

⅓ cup sugar

1 cup boiling water

½ cup brandy*

½ cup light rum*

Mint sprigs for garnish

1. Thaw frozen berries. Reserve a few fresh berries for garnish. Place berries in blender container and blend until pureed.

2. Strain puree, reserving juice and discarding seeds.

3. Make syrup by adding sugar to boiling water, stirring until sugar dissolves.

4. Combine reserved juice, sugar syrup, brandy, and rum. Cover and refrigerate.

5. Serve over ice cubes in small glasses or cups. Garnish with mint sprigs and a few fresh raspberries.

Makes 6 to 8 4-ounce servings.

*If you wish the drink to be non-alcoholic, use ½ cup tea instead of brandy and ½ cup apple juice instead of light rum.

Appetizing Angels on Horseback— grilled oysters and bacon on toast garnished with lemon wedges, lemon leaves and oyster shells—are displayed below.

Angels on Horseback

These intriguing morsels are indeed heaven-sent for oyster lovers.

8 slices bacon

16 shucked oysters*

4 slices bread

2 tablespoons butter, softened

1 teaspoon finely chopped parsley

½ teaspoon anchovy paste,

    optional

Lemon wedges, parsley sprigs, and

    red leaf lettuce for garnish

1. Preheat oven to 400°. Cut bacon in half crosswise. Wrap each oyster in half slice of bacon; secure with wooden picks.

2. Arrange on rack in shallow baking pan. Bake about 10 minutes, until bacon is crisp.

3. Meanwhile, toast bread. Blend butter with parsley and anchovy paste, if used.

4. Butter toast with seasoned butter. Trim crusts if desired and cut each slice into four triangles. Place one oyster on each triangle. Serve hot, with lemon wedges. Garnish platter with parsley sprigs and/or red-leaf lettuce leaves.

Makes 16 appetizer servings.

*For "Devils on Horseback," instead of oysters substitute whole pitted dates or prunes.

Butter-braised Chicken with Garden Herbs

A savory recipe for chicken using abundant herbs.

2 3- to 3½-pound broiler-fryer chickens, quartered

½ cup butter

1 teaspoon dried or 1 tablespoon fresh rosemary

1 teaspoon dried or 1 tablespoon fresh sage

1 teaspoon dried or 1 tablespoon fresh chervil

1 teaspoon dried or 1 tablespoon fresh tarragon

1 teaspoon dried or 1 tablespoon fresh thyme

½ cup coarsely chopped parsley

4 leafy celery tops, cut into 2-inch lengths

1 large onion, quartered

1 teaspoon salt, or to taste

¾ teaspoon freshly ground black pepper

1 cup dry white wine

½ cup chicken broth

1. Rinse chicken in cold water and pat dry.

2. In large covered roaster, melt butter. Add rosemary, sage, chervil, tarragon, and thyme.

3. Add chicken pieces, turning in herb butter to coat on all sides. Sprinkle with parsley, celery, onion, salt, and pepper. Pour wine and chicken broth over all.

4. Bring mixture to a boil on top of range, reduce heat, cover, and simmer for 1 hour or until chicken is fork tender. Baste occasionally with pan juices. (If you wish you can bake in oven at 350° for 1 hour, removing cover during last 20 to 30 minutes to allow chicken to brown.)

6. Arrange chicken on serving platter with a few tablespoons cooking liquid poured over. Strain remaining cooking liquid and serve in a sauceboat on the side as a gravy.

Makes 6 to 8 servings.

Celery Victor St. Francis

Celery Victor St. Francis was originated by Chef Victor Hirtzler for the St. Francis Hotel in San Francisco. The St. Francis opened in 1904 and was the outstanding place to have lunch.

CELERY

6 stalks celery, halved crosswise

2 cups chicken broth

2 bay leaves

½ teaspoon freshly ground black pepper

¼ teaspoon crushed red pepper
　　flakes

½ teaspoon dried tarragon

2 cloves

DRESSING

½ teaspoon salt, or to taste

½ teaspoon freshly ground black pepper

¼ teaspoon dry mustard

¼ teaspoon tarragon

1 teaspoon minced green onion

3 tablespoons white wine vinegar

6 tablespoons olive oil

GARNISH

1 4-ounce jar pimientos, drained

1 2-ounce can anchovy fillets

2 teaspoons capers

Parsley sprigs

1. Place celery in saucepan or skillet and add chicken broth, bay leaves, black pepper, red pepper, tarragon, and cloves. Bring to a boil, cover, reduce heat, and simmer for about 8 minutes, until tender. Let cool in broth, refrigerate until cold.

2. Drain celery and place in deep serving dish. (Save broth for another use—as a soup base, for instance.)

3. Make dressing by combining salt, pepper, dry mustard, tarragon, and green onion. Add vinegar and oil and beat with wire whisk or fork. Pour over celery, coating well.

4. Cut pimientos into strips and arrange on celery lengthwise. Place anchovy fillets in a crisscross arrangement on celery. Sprinkle capers over all. Decorate with parsley. Cover with plastic wrap and refrigerate.

Makes 6 side-dish servings.

VICTORIAN AFTERNOONS

B Y VICTORIAN TIMES, THE MIDDAY LUNCH OR LUNCHEON WAS FAIRLY WELL ESTABLISHED. WHAT IT WAS CALLED WAS SUBJECT TO SOME ODD VAGARIES OF FASHION. AFTER DINNER CAME TO BE SERVED IN THE LATE AFTERNOON OR EVENING, THE OLD WORD *NUNCHEON* (LITERALLY, A "NOON DRINK") WAS APPROPRIATED FOR A LIGHT MIDDAY MEAL BETWEEN BREAKFAST AND DINNER. BY THE 1820s OR SO, THIS MEAL CAME TO BE CALLED LUNCH OR LUNCHEON.

WHATEVER ITS NAME, THE MEAL WAS NO SANDWICH AND COFFEE, AT LEAST NOT WHEN TAKEN IN COMPANY. A VICTORIAN BOOK ON ENTERTAINING GIVES A BILL OF FARE FOR A LADIES' SPRING LUNCHEON THAT CONSISTS OF CLAMS, CONSOMMÉ, *CÔTELETTES DE CERVELLE À LA*

Cardinal (calves' brains) with cucumbers, "little ducks with fresh mushrooms," artichokes, sweet-breads à la Richelieu, asparagus with hollandaise sauce, pâté de foie gras, roast snipe, lettuce and tomato salad, ice cream "in form of nightingales' nests," strawberries, "nougat cake," and coffee—accompanied by chablis, champagne, claret, and liqueurs with the dessert.

Such meals were not—one hopes—everyday fare. But after luncheon, which was usually eaten sometime between twelve thirty and one thirty, a lady would put on afternoon dress and embark on the ritual of formal calls. From three to six in the afternoon, ladies would call upon their acquaintances—or those whom they hoped to make their acquaintances. If the lady called upon was "not at home," visiting cards would be left; if she was, the caller would sit down for a precisely decreed period (usually fifteen minutes) of social chit-chat.

Winter or summer, town or country, four or five o'clock tea was inevitable in England and quite common in America. It might be simply tea and toast, muffins, or scones, taken en famille or with friends who happened to drop in. Or it might be a formal reception, in which a new bride entertained for the first time under her own roof, a hostess introduced a friend or relative from out of town to local society, or some prominent member of the community or visiting lion was honored. Teas and afternoon socializing were a time for conviviality in good company—a tradition in entertaining we would do well to revive.

SUNDAY AFTERNOON SOCIAL

Garden parties are becoming very fashionable at watering-places, in rural cities, and at country houses which are accessible to a town.
— M. E. N. Sherwood, *The Art of Entertaining,* 1892

Though strong notions of what was permissible on Sunday continued in Victorian times, most people considered some pastimes innocent and acceptable. Eating, drinking (at least the drinking of tea—the total abstinence movement was beginning to make its influence felt), and conversation were among them, and so the Sunday afternoon social became popular. It offered an occasion for parents and children, uncles and aunts, grandparents and friends of mixed "ages and stages" to come together in relaxed conviviality. In fall or winter it might take the form of a high tea. With the lamps lit and the curtains drawn against the outside gloom, the family and guests would gather around the fire. Cakes, small sandwiches, and possibly a more substantial dish or two would be served, and the *mater familias* would pour tea.

In the country, all kinds of activities were planned for summer Sunday afternoons, from family teas on the front porch with only a guest or two to a grand reception on the village green for a local hero or dignitary. Such events might be held after the last Sunday school session of the year—indeed, "Sunday school picnic" remains in the language as a type of innocent frivolity—or to celebrate a graduation. Balloon ascensions were another popular occasion for an *al fresco* meal enjoyed as spectators waited for the wind to be just right.

Emerson wrote, "The ornament of a house is the friends who frequent it." The arrival of friends from out of town was an important social occasion—one to which neighbors and the local clergy might be invited. Fashions, recipes, gossip, and news of the world at large were exchanged.

The food would be simple, but colorful and appetizing to look at, and would be arranged on long cloth-covered tables in the open air or, if the weather looked threatening, in a tent. Guests would wear elegant but comfortable clothes; if the affair was held right after church, their "Sunday-go-to-meeting dress." Men sported straw boaters, women large flattering picture hats. Everyone wore light pastel shades, cream, and white. Children, too, were outfitted in their best, the girls in soft dropped-waist dresses with big ribbons in their long hair, while the boys wore shirts, sometimes jackets, soft ties, shorts, and knee socks. Children would be adjured to be on their best behavior, but after the inevitable games of hide-and-seek or tag, there would surely be a few lost ribbons and torn frocks, and perhaps even a skinned knee or two.

⚘

Our menu is a blend of typical English and American dishes. Cucumber and watercress sandwiches are quintessentially British, and curry was more common there too. But the elaborate layer cakes are very American; in Victorian England, "cake" nearly always meant fruitcake, which was a tea-time staple.

For your own summer Sunday party, make the table setting as light and delicate as possible. Cover the table with a pale mint green or blue cloth; top that with a white or ecru cutwork or lace cloth. Use fanciful floral and bird-embroidered napkins, rolling and tying each with a ribbon. Center the table with a mixed bouquet of wild flowers: Queen Anne's lace, black-eyed susans, clover, daylilies, and grasses.

Serve the drinks in tall Collins glasses, big brandy snifters, and generously scaled pressed glass tumblers. Garnish all drinks as prettily as you can with fresh mint, pansies, nasturtiums, and violets. For clear drinks freeze tiny edible flowers in ice cubes as an engaging touch. Note: take care not to use garden flowers that have been exposed to *any* kind of garden chemicals.

Arrange sweets or cookies on white or floral decorated plates.

In South Carolina, below, inviting summer coolers are served in an exotic jungle atmosphere. The refreshing drinks include iced tea with mint and lemon, Ginger Pear Delight, Chocolate Mint Cream, and Berry-Thyme Cooler.

MENU

SUNDAY AFTERNOON SOCIAL

Assorted Tea Sandwiches: Cucumber, Chicken, Watercress, Ham, Nutted Cheese

Pâte à Choux Puffs with Curried Chicken Salad*

Banana Apricot Cake*

Princess Cake*

Glazed Fruit Tarts*

Fresh Lemon Ice Cream*

Old-fashioned Lemonade*   Daiquiris*   Tea   Coffee

Ginger Pear Delight*   Chocolate Mint Cream*   Berry-Thyme Cooler*

*Recipe given

Pâte à Choux Puffs with Curried Chicken Salad

These delightful little puffs with a savory filling are probably British in origin.

PÂTE À CHOUX

1 cup water or milk

⅓ cup butter

1 cup all-purpose flour

⅛ teaspoon salt

4 eggs

FILLING

2 cups finely chopped cooked chicken

1 cup finely chopped celery

½ cup finely chopped peeled apple

⅓ cup finely sliced green onions

1 tablespoon dried currants

1 cup mayonnaise

½ teaspoon salt

¼ teaspoon freshly ground black
  pepper

Dash cayenne pepper

2 teaspoons curry powder

½ cup chopped chutney and syrup

Green celery tops for garnish

1. Preheat oven to 400°. Have all ingredients measured and ready at hand.

2. Heat water or milk and butter to a boil in 3-quart saucepan. Add flour and salt all at once and stir vigorously with a wooden spoon. Beat over medium heat until the paste becomes dry and leaves the sides of the pan. Do not overcook or over stir!

3. Remove pan from heat. Add eggs one at a time, beating vigorously after each addition.

4. Using a teaspoon, scoop out heaping teaspoonfuls of dough onto greased baking pan. Allow for spreading. (Or fill pastry bag and pipe small mounds using ½-inch plain tip.)

5. Before baking sprinkle with a little cold water. This helps create steam.

6. Bake at 400° for 10 minutes; reduce heat to 350° and bake 20 minutes longer. When done, puffs will have puffed up and be firm to the touch.

7. Cool puffs completely. When ready to fill, cut off tops crosswise.

FILLING

1. In large bowl mix all ingredients except celery tops. Stir thoroughly to combine.

2. Refrigerate, covered, if not serving immediately.

3. Fill each puff with about 1 tablespoon filling and top with puff top. Garnish platter with green celery tops. Refrigerate if not serving immediately.

Makes 3½ cups filling, 36 small puffs.

Note: This tasty filling is also good in tea sandwiches. However, if using for sandwiches the chutney should be drained and only the solid chutney fruits used, not the liquid.

The unabashed pleasure of a summer afternoon lies in the visual delight of seasonal flowers and tempting Banana Apricot Cake, cold Old-fashioned Lemonade, and Glazed Fruit Tarts, below.

Banana Apricot Cake

Showy to look at and easy to construct.

2 8- or 9-inch cake layers (see recipe for Two-Egg Yellow Cake on page 69)

1 cup apricot jam

3 tablespoons Grand Marnier or apricot brandy

2 bananas

1 cup heavy cream

2 tablespoons confectioners' sugar

½ teaspoon vanilla extract

6 to 8 canned apricot halves or pitted whole apricots for garnish

1. Cake layers should be cool and brushed free of excess crumbs.

2. In 1-quart saucepan heat apricot jam until melted, stirring constantly. Stir in Grand Marnier or apricot brandy.

3. Brush top and sides of layers with apricot glaze.

4. Slice bananas and place on top of each layer.

5. Whip cream until stiff. Stir in confectioners' sugar and vanilla extract.

6. Place one layer on serving plate. Spoon ½ cup of whipped cream over top of layer. Place second layer on top and spread remaining whipped cream over it. Garnish with apricot halves.

7. Refrigerate until ready to serve. Best when served soon after making.

Makes 8 servings.

Princess Cake

A party cake of Swedish origin.

SPONGE CAKE

4 large eggs (2 whole, 2 separated)	¼ cup potato starch
⅔ cup sugar	1 teaspoon grated lemon zest
⅓ cup all-purpose flour	2 tablespoons bread crumbs

FILLING

2 eggs	1 cup boiling milk or cream
2 tablespoons sugar	½ cup heavy cream
1 tablespoon all-purpose flour	1 teaspoon vanilla extract

ICING

1 cup ground almonds	½ teaspoon almond extract
1 cup confectioners' sugar	Green food coloring
2 to 4 tablespoons heavy cream	Whipped cream for garnish
	Few raspberries or strawberries for garnish

1. Preheat oven to 350°. In large bowl, using electric mixer, beat 2 eggs and 2 egg yolks together with sugar until fluffy.

2. On sheet of wax paper combine flour, potato starch, and lemon zest. Add to egg-sugar mixture and beat at medium speed, blending well.

3. In separate bowl using clean beaters, beat the 2 egg whites until they form stiff peaks; gently fold into egg mixture.

4. Sprinkle a well-buttered 9-inch springform pan with fine dry bread crumbs. Pour batter into prepared pan and bake at 350° for about 30 to 40 minutes or until cake springs back when lightly touched in center. Do not over bake. Cool on rack.

FILLING

1. In small bowl, using wire whisk, beat eggs, sugar, and flour together smoothly.

2. Add boiling milk or cream, beating as you pour. Return mixture to saucepan and cook, stirring constantly with wire whisk, until mixture thickens and comes to a boil. Chill, covered, in refrigerator until cold.

3. Beat heavy cream until stiff. Beat chilled egg mixture with wire whisk. Add whipped cream and vanilla to egg mixture. Refrigerate until ready to use.

ICING

1. In a bowl, mix ground almonds with sugar; add cream and stir until mixture

is fluffy. Add almond extract.

2. Add the tiniest drop of food coloring to mixture to tint a pale light green.

3. Press mixture into a ball, place on sheet of plastic wrap and wrap securely; flatten into a thick pancake.

ASSEMBLY

1. Cut sponge cake crosswise into 2 or 3 layers, as desired. Spread most of the filling between layers; reserve enough to cover top of cake. Refrigerate.

2. Roll icing mixture between 2 sheets of wax paper until very thin, making a 12-inch circle. Cover the top of the cake and spread down over sides, pressing icing gently but firmly to attach to cake.

3. Dust lightly with confectioners' sugar and garnish top with rosettes of whipped cream and berries as desired. Refrigerate cake until ready to serve.

Makes 8 servings.

Note: if you do not wish to make the almond paste icing from scratch, buy an 8-ounce package of ready-made almond paste and roll out as directed above.

Reminiscent of grandmother's own version, this layered beauty, Banana Apricot Cake, above, goes a step further with the addition of jam and liqueur.

Two-Egg Yellow Cake

A basic recipe for a butter cake.

½ cup butter	2 teaspoons baking powder
1 cup sugar	½ teaspoon salt
2 eggs	¾ cup milk
2 cups sifted cake flour	1 teaspoon vanilla extract

1. Preheat oven to 350°. In bowl, using electric mixer, beat butter until softened. At medium speed add sugar gradually, creaming until mixture is fluffy.

2. Add eggs and beat in thoroughly at high speed.

3. Sift flour, baking powder, and salt together. Add flour mixture at low speed in thirds, alternating with milk and ending with flour. Add vanilla. Clean beaters and sides of bowl with scraper.

4. Turn batter into two greased and floured 8- or 9-inch layer cake pans. Bake in 350° oven for about 25 minutes, or until cake springs back in center when lightly pressed with fingertip.

5. Cook 4 or 5 minutes on rack, loosen at edges, and invert cakes onto rack to cool completely.

Makes 2 layers.

Glazed Fruit Tarts

Classic and jewel-like, these beauties are sure to please.

PÂTE BRISÉE

2½ cups all-purpose flour

1 teaspoon salt, or to taste

1 teaspoon sugar, optional

1 cup very cold sweet butter, cut
in small pieces

¼ to ½ cup ice water

CREAM FILLING (CRÈME PÂTISSIÈRE)

1 cup milk

½ vanilla bean or 1 teaspoon vanilla
extract

4 tablespoons sugar

3 large egg yolks

2 tablespoons cornstarch

Fresh fruits: red raspberries,
strawberries, seedless green
grapes

1½ cups crab apple jelly

1 to 2 tablespoons Grand Marnier,
peach brandy, apricot brandy,
or kirsch

TART SHELLS

1. Put flour, salt, and sugar in the bowl of food processor.

2. Add the butter and process for about 8 to 10 seconds or until mixture is like coarse meal. If you are mixing by hand, combine dry ingredients in a large bowl. Cut in the butter with a pastry blender or two knives until mixture looks like coarse meal.

3. Add ice water one teaspoonful at a time through feed tube with motor running. Add just enough water so that dough clumps together.

4. Turn dough out onto large sheet of plastic wrap and fold sides of wrap over dough. Flatten dough with your hands to make a large, thick pancake (to make rolling out easier). Refrigerate for an hour or two.

5. Grease 12 2- to 3-inch tart pans or spray with vegetable cooking spray.

6. On a lightly floured board, roll out dough to ⅛-inch thickness. Cut circles of dough 1 inch larger than diameter of tart pans. Fit dough circles into tart pans, pressing lightly with fingers to fit. Trim off edges of dough—or fold over, pressing against sides of pans to make a thicker, firmer rim.

7. To bake, prick bottom of dough with fork in several places to prevent bubbles. Place a 4-inch square of foil in each tart pan and fill with dry beans, rice, or pie weights.

8. Place tarts on baking sheet and bake at 425° for about 10 minutes, until pastry is golden. Remove from oven, place on rack, and cool 5 minutes; remove foil and beans. Allow to cool completely before filling.

Makes 12 2- to 3-inch tart shells.

FILLING

1. Heat milk with vanilla bean and 2 tablespoons sugar, just to the boiling point. Remove from heat.

2. In bowl, beat egg yolks with remaining 2 tablespoons sugar until thick. This will take several minutes. Add cornstarch to the beaten yolk mixture and whisk until blended.

3. Remove vanilla bean from milk or add vanilla extract at this point if you are using it. Slowly beat half of the hot milk into the beaten yolk mixture. Return to saucepan with remaining hot milk and rapidly bring to a boil, stirring vigorously with wire whisk.

4. Remove custard from heat and pour into bowl. Cover with plastic wrap and refrigerate immediately to chill thoroughly. Stir several times during this time so cooling will be faster.

5. Spoon about 2 to 3 tablespoons crème pâtissière into each tart shell. Arrange on top fruit that is dry or well drained and patted dry. Place fruits as closely and as decoratively as possible.

6. In small saucepan heat jelly with liqueur or brandy until melted.

7. Spoon or brush melted jelly over fruits to glaze. Cool. Best served promptly after making, otherwise refrigerate until serving.

Makes 12 2- to 3-inch tarts.

Old-fashioned Lemonade

Lemonade was an exceedingly popular summer drink in Victorian times.

Juice of 6 lemons (1 cup)

¾ cup sugar, or to taste

4 cups cold water

1 lemon cut into thin cartwheel slices

Ice cubes

1. In a large pitcher, combine the lemon juice and sugar; stir to dissolve the sugar.

2. Add remaining ingredients and stir well.

Makes 6 cups (6 8-ounce servings).

VARIATIONS:

Pink Lemonade: Add a few drops of red food coloring or grenadine syrup.

Honey Lemonade: Substitute honey to taste for the sugar.

Mint: Add ¼ cup chopped or bruised mint leaves to lemonade. Garnish with mint sprigs.

Daiquiris

An easy-to-make, refreshing drink.

1 cup crushed ice

⅓ cup light rum

1 tablespoon freshly squeezed lime
  juice

2 teaspoons sugar (use superfine
  sugar if available)

1. Combine all ingredients in container of electric blender and cover; blend until smooth.

2. Serve in chilled stemmed cocktail glasses.

Makes 2 drinks.

*To make strawberry or banana daiquiris, add ½ cup sliced strawberries or ½ cup sliced bananas to above ingredients. Blend as directed.

Ginger Pear Delight

Candied ginger gives piquance to the pears.

¼ cup sugar

½ vanilla bean or 1 teaspoon vanilla
  extract

1 pound firm, ripe pears, peeled,
  cored, and sliced

¼ cup chopped crystallized ginger

1. Bring 1 cup water, sugar, and vanilla bean to a boil, stirring until sugar dissolves.

2. Add pear slices and ginger and return to a boil. Reduce heat, cover, and boil gently 5 minutes. Cool. May be served as a dessert or a late morning breakfast fruit.

Makes 2½ cups.

To make Delight Cooler: Place ½ cup Ginger Pear Delight fruit and syrup and ½ cup apricot nectar in blender. Cover, and blend until smooth. Pour over ice in tall glass. Garnish with pitted fresh apricot or mint leaves. Makes 1 drink.

On a shady Victorian porch in Greenwood, South Carolina, below, a gleaming silver serving tray makes cooling drinks appear even cooler. From left to right: minted lemon iced tea, Chocolate Mint Cream with whimsical umbrellas, and a slushy Ginger Pear Delight.

Chocolate Mint Cream

Mint and chocolate are a natural taste combination.

⅓ cup mint jelly	6 tablespoons milk or half-and-
Ice cubes	half
6 tablespoons chocolate syrup	Chilled club soda or seltzer
	Mint leaves for garnish

1. In a small saucepan heat mint jelly with 2 tablespoons water, stirring until jelly melts and mixture boils. Cool.

2. For each drink fill tall 12-ounce glass with ice cubes and 2 tablespoons mint syrup, 2 tablespoons chocolate syrup, and 2 tablespoons milk or half-and-half. Fill with club soda and stir.

3. Garnish with mint leaves and a beverage stirrer.

Makes 3 drinks.

Berry-Thyme Cooler

The combination of sweet with the bite of the herb is the flavor secret.

Raspberry, blackberry, or currant syrup

Fresh thyme leaves

Ice cubes

Apple juice or cider

Club soda or seltzer

Fresh berries, apple slices, and

    thyme sprigs for garnish

1. To make 1 drink, muddle 2 tablespoons berry syrup and ¼ teaspoon thyme leaves in tall 12-ounce glass.

2. Add ice cubes, fill glass halfway with apple juice, then top with club soda. Garnish with a few fresh berries, an apple slice, and a sprig of fresh thyme. Make quantity as desired.

Fresh Lemon Ice Cream

Creamy, easy, and pretty to look at.

2 cups heavy cream or half-and-half

1 cup sugar

1 tablespoon freshly grated lemon zest

⅓ cup freshly squeezed lemon

    juice

7 to 10 scalloped lemon shells,

    optional

1. In large bowl, combine cream or half-and-half and sugar; stir until sugar dissolves.

2. Blend in lemon zest and juice. Pour into shallow pan (an 8 × 8-inch square pan is fine).

3. Freeze until firm, about 4 hours. Serve in hollowed-out lemon shells or small dessert glasses.

Makes 3 cups (6 ½-cup servings).

CROQUET PARTY

"If it's fine, I'm going to pitch my tent in Longmeadow, and row up the whole crew to lunch and croquet—have a fire, make messes, gypsy fashion, and all sorts of larks."
—Louisa May Alcott, Little Women

Gently rolling lawns, whether at southern mansions, midwestern carpenter gothic houses, or stately English country houses, were the perfect setting for croquet. This game has been said to derive from a French peasant pastime of the thirteenth century called *paille maille,* which eventually evolved into the sixteenth- and seventeenth-century sport of pall mall. Croquet as we know it is thought to have been brought from Ireland to England about 1840, and thence to the United States, where the New York Croquet Club was organized in 1867. The game was extremely popular—as it required no great strength or exertion, the most fragile of Victorian ladies could play it. But as it rewarded what we would now call eye-hand and hand-mind coordination (in which respect it greatly resembles billiards), it offered sufficient challenge to the gentlemen. And, in an era when exclusively masculine and exclusively feminine activities were more and more common, it was an acceptable pastime for men and women to indulge in together.

The sunny lawn of The Mansion, right, a Victorian bed and breakfast in Rock City Falls, New York, is the perfect setting for croquet and hence a Croquet Party. The drooping branches of a tiger-tail spruce provide a gentle shade for the spread feast.

A leisurely golden summer afternoon was the favored occasion. There was no special "croquet costume," as there was for yachting and would later be for tennis. Ladies wore their usual afternoon dresses, long-sleeved, long-skirted, and panniered, bustled, or crinolined as the whims of fashion decreed, and hats or bonnets. Gentlemen wore trousers and jackets, shirts, ties, and hats (often straw boaters); they might doff their hats but not, it would appear from contemporary illustrations, their jackets.

Various sets of rules and patterns of play have been used at different times and places—and their relative merits hotly contested. After the game—or sometimes before—a picnic lunch would be enjoyed outdoors, on a cloth or blanket or rug spread out on the grass or on a white-clothed table under a tree. Cool, light salads were popular (but "salad" in Victorian days more often meant a mixture of meat or seafood, bound with mayonnaise or boiled dressing, than the mixed greens of today). Chicken was a favorite, either in a salad, *en gelée,* or just sliced cold. Lettuce or other greens there might be, especially in America. Sliced tomatoes, rolls, and finger sandwiches were also served. Croquet might not be strenuous, but a great deal of talking—about the game or other topics—went on, and the players would work up a thirst that had to be quenched. Tea or coffee would be made over a spirit lamp or a fire, but varied cool drinks were also in order, perhaps double lemon punch, a refreshing brew of lemon verbena leaves, cooled black tea, ginger beer, and sliced lemons. A modern version might be a raspberry ginger ale with a few fresh berries and sprigs of mint as a garnish.

MENU

CROQUET PARTY

Assorted Bread and Herb Butter Finger Sandwiches

Pâté and Chutney Triangle Sandwiches

Jellied Chicken Salad*

Fresh Dill Dressing*

Sliced Garden Tomatoes with Chive Vinegar

Fresh Fruit Skewers

Brownies

White Wine and Kir Punch

Lemonade with Mint

*Recipe given

Jellied Chicken Salad

Molding food into elaborate tin or tin-lined copper molds was very popular during Victorian times. In her 1896 Pratt Institute graduation thesis, "A Model School Kitchen," Miss Emily Merrill recommended the provision of nineteen molds—sixteen small and two large jelly molds and one large ice cream mold.

CHICKEN

5- to 6-pound stewing or roasting chicken	3 sprigs parsley
2 onions stuck with 3 cloves each	½ teaspoon whole black peppercorns
2 bay leaves	2 teaspoons salt
2 stalks celery with leaves	3 envelopes gelatin
1 large carrot, quartered	

GARNISH

Small lettuce leaves	Radish roses
Blanched broccoli florets	Capers
Artichoke hearts	

1. Rinse chicken under cold running water. Reserve giblets for another use.

2. Place chicken in stockpot or Dutch oven. Add 1½ quarts water, onions, bay leaves, celery, carrot, parsley, peppercorns, and salt. Bring to a boil, reduce heat, cover, and allow to boil gently for about 1 hour or until chicken is very tender and beginning to fall away from the bones.

3. Strain chicken and broth in large strainer or colander. Discard vegetables.

4. Refrigerate broth and chicken separately until chicken is cool enough to handle.

5. Skin and bone chicken. Discard skin and bones. Chop chicken.

6. Remove fat from surface of chicken broth. Ladle 1 cup of chicken broth into small bowl and sprinkle gelatin over it to soften. Measure 1¾ quarts chicken broth into saucepan and add softened gelatin. Heat to a boil, stirring until gelatin is completely dissolved.

7. Refrigerate chicken broth until consistency of raw egg white. Combine soft gelled chicken broth with chopped chicken and mix well. Taste, adding more salt and pepper if desired.

8. Divide mixture between two 9 × 5 × 3-inch loaf pans. Refrigerate to chill and gel completely.

9. To serve: Unmold each loaf and cut into 1-inch-thick slices. Arrange slices on platter; garnish with small lettuce leaves, chilled blanched broccoli florets, artichoke hearts, radish roses, and capers. Serve with Fresh Dill Dressing.

Makes 2 loaves (8 servings per loaf).

Fresh Dill Dressing

This fresh and tangy dressing should be kept well chilled if served outdoors.

1½ cups mayonnaise

1½ cups yogurt

2 tablespoons Dijon mustard

1½ cups chopped fresh dill

1½ teaspoons salt, or to taste

½ teaspoon ground white pepper

1½ tablespoons lemon juice

Combine all ingredients in a large bowl and mix well. Use as a dressing for Jellied Chicken Salad.

Makes about 3 cups (16 servings).

Who wouldn't enjoy this menu, right, from a hamper: Pâté and Chutney Triangle Sandwiches, Sliced Garden Tomatoes with Chive Vinegar, Jellied Chicken Salad, Fresh Dill Dressing, ice cream watermelon bombe, and iced tea.

WINTER-WHITE DESSERT PARTY

Of late it has been the fashion to have one prevailing color. . .
—Mary Ronald, *Century Cook Book,* 1895

In the 1890s, when this idea was the rage, the one color prevailed not merely in the decorations but in the food itself. The color would be chosen to complement the theme of the meal. Mrs. Ronald suggested white for a bride, red for Harvard students or graduates, and "yellow to those with Princeton affiliations" (in fact, orange is Princeton's color). An all-white party makes an excellent theme for a winter event, both because of its likeness to snow and because it lightens up the whole house. Other occasions for which it would be appropriate are a wedding anniversary or a reception after a play or concert.

We might combine a menu with white as the dominant color with the older tradition of the New Year's at-home. This custom, said to have been started by the Dutch families of New York, by Revolutionary times had spread to other parts of the Colonies. President George Washington began the custom of a presidential open house on New Year's Day; John Adams combined the New Year's reception of 1801 with the official opening of the White House.

By Victorian times, "at home" was the standard phrase used on invitations to afternoon receptions or teas. Such invitations did not require a reply, as the food was served buffet style and was always plentiful. The menu might be merely tea, wine, and cakes, or might encompass a substantial cold collation. The New Year's at-home continued popular. At one point, however, things got out of hand: newspapers would publish lists of which hostesses would be "at home" at what hours on New Year's Day, and rowdy young men would make the rounds, stopping for food and a glass—or two or more—of wine or punch at each. By the end of the century, the hostesses had had enough and ceased to print their "at home" schedule in the papers. The New Year's at-home continued, but with only invited guests.

For your New Year's at-home of white desserts, cover the table with a white linen cloth—damask would be perfect. In the center place a bowl of roses—white or varying shades from white to cream. Place a candelabrum with white candles on either side of the flowers. The Victorians loved ribbons, so tie a long-streamered white bow around the rose bowl. The streamers should be three to four feet long, and can gracefully unfurl themselves across the table, on which white rose petals and tiny buds can be scattered. Choose silver, white, or the palest of pastel serving dishes. Vary their heights if possible by using footed stands and compote dishes.

If the event is a very large and festive one, have a florist fashion a long green garland (at New Year's it might be of pine, yew, or other evergreens) and attach baby's breath at regular intervals along its length. This green roping can be attached to a staircase banister, or draped over doorways or around a fireplace. Place white candles in groups of varying heights, and tie long ribbons in bows around a candlestick or two, letting the ends fall softly in streamers.

The ultimate in an all-white dessert party is a wedding reception. This Victorian wedding cake, right, created by Cile Burbidge, is presented with ribbon-tied boxes of groom's cake for each guest to take home "to dream on." The spectacular setting is the House of Seven Gables in Salem, Massachusetts.

MENU

WINTER-WHITE DESSERT PARTY

White Grape Tart with Chocolate-Nut Crust*

Champagne Sorbet*

Peach Blitz Kuchen*

Lace-topped Gingerbread with Warm Lemon Sauce

Baked Alaska* with Brandied Apricot Sauce*

*Recipe given

White Grape Tart with Chocolate-Nut Crust

The filling for the White Grape Tart is based upon the time-honored Bavarian Cream recipe which always contained gelatin, eggs, sugar, and cream. Make this refrigerator dessert one day before serving.

CRUST

1½ cups chocolate wafer crumbs

¼ cup confectioners' sugar

¼ cup finely chopped walnuts or pecans

6 tablespoons butter, melted

FILLING

1 tablespoon unflavored gelatin

½ cup milk

¼ cup crab apple jelly

2 tablespoons sugar

4 egg yolks

⅛ teaspoon salt

1 teaspoon vanilla extract

1 cup heavy cream

1 cup seedless green grapes, washed, dried, and halved

GARNISH

1 egg white

3 to 5 small clusters of seedless green grapes

¼ cup granulated sugar

½ cup heavy cream

CRUST

1. Preheat oven to 350°. In medium bowl, combine chocolate wafer crumbs, confections' sugar, and nuts.

2. Add melted butter and stir until well mixed.

3. Sprinkle crumb mixture over bottom of 9-inch pie pan. Press evenly on bottom and up sides of pie pan, making a crust.

4. Bake crust for 10 minutes. Remove from oven and cool.

FILLING

1. Sprinkle gelatin over 2 tablespoons cold water to soften.

2. Heat milk in small saucepan until a rim of fine bubbles appears around edge of pan. Add jelly and stir until jelly melts. Remove from heat.

3. In small bowl, using mixer or wire whisk, beat sugar, egg yolks, and salt.

4. Pour a little of the hot milk mixture over egg-sugar mixture, beating rapidly. Slowly pour in remaining milk mixture, beating constantly.

5. Pour mixture into top of double boiler and cook over boiling water, stirring until mixture begins to thicken. Add softened gelatin and stir until dissolved. Add vanilla.

(recipe continued next page)

6. Pour mixture into bowl, cover, and refrigerate until mixture is almost set.

7. Whip cream until it holds a soft shape and fold into chilled mixture. Fold in halved grapes.

8. Pour mixture into cool pie crust, mounding high in center. Refrigerate until firm, about 6 hours or overnight.

GARNISH

1. Beat egg white with fork until frothy. Brush egg white lightly on grape clusters. Roll grape clusters in granulated sugar and place on plate to dry.

2. When ready to serve, whip ½ cup heavy cream until stiff and spread lightly on top of pie. Arrange sugar-frosted grape clusters on top of pie.

Makes 8 servings.

Champagne Sorbet

A delightful excess, especially made with pink champagne. Select your prettiest glasses to serve it in; they need not all match.

1 cup sugar	2 egg whites
1½ cups pink champagne	3 tablespoons superfine sugar
4 tablespoons lemon juice	Pink champagne (1 split bottle)
⅛ teaspoon cream of tartar	for garnish

1. In small saucepan, combine 1 cup sugar and 1 cup water. Heat to a boil, stirring until sugar dissolves. Boil 5 minutes, covered, without stirring. Cool.

2. Pour sugar syrup into bowl. Add 1½ cups champagne and lemon juice. Pour mixture into an ice cream maker and freeze according to manufacturer's directions until soft-frozen.

3. In bowl, add cream of tartar to egg whites and beat until foamy. Gradually add superfine sugar, beating hard after each addition. Continue to beat until stiff peaks form when beater is raised.

4. Fold this meringue into the soft-frozen mixture. Pack into a container, cover, and freeze until firm.

5. Serve with a tablespoon or two of champagne poured over each serving.

Makes 8 servings.

Peach Blitz Kuchen

A variation on an old German recipe that uses fresh fruit to good advantage.

CAKE

1 cup butter	1 teaspoon vanilla extract
1 cup sugar	2 cups all-purpose flour
1 egg	2 teaspoons baking powder
3 egg yolks	¼ teaspoon salt
1 teaspoon grated lemon zest	⅔ cup milk

MERINGUE

¼ teaspoon cream of tartar	½ cup chopped walnuts, pecans,
3 egg whites	or almonds
½ cup sugar, preferably superfine	

TOPPING

2 to 3 cups sliced, peeled sweetened	½ to 1 cup heavy cream
peaches (fresh, frozen, or canned),	1 tablespoon confectioners' sugar,
sliced strawberries, or whole	optional
raspberries (fresh or frozen)	

1. Preheat oven to 350°. Grease and flour two 8-inch cake pans. In large bowl, using electric mixer, cream the butter and add sugar gradually, beating until fluffy.

2. Beat in egg, yolks, lemon zest, and vanilla.

3. Sift flour, baking powder, and salt together.

4. Add the sifted dry ingredients and milk to egg yolk mixture alternately, beginning and ending with the flour mixture.

5. Divide batter between the two prepared cake pans and spread evenly.

6. Make meringue: In large bowl, using electric mixer, add cream of tartar to egg whites and beat until frothy.

7. Gradually add ½ cup sugar, beating until stiff peaks form.

8. Spread meringue lightly over batter in two cake pans. Sprinkle with nuts. Bake for 30 to 35 minutes or until cake tests done and meringue is pale gold. Cool on rack.

9. When cake is cool, carefully remove from pans. Place one layer (meringue side up) on cake plate and top with half the fruit.

10. Whip cream until stiff. Sweeten if desired with 1 tablespoon confectioners' sugar. Spoon one-third of the whipped cream over fruit on first layer. Top with second layer (meringue side up). Spoon on whipped cream and top with fruit. Makes 8 to 10 servings.

A polished mahogany chair gleams and a shallow bowl holds a cluster of soft pink and cream roses, opposite page. A regal-looking cake, above, this Peach Blitz Kuchen has been baked half in a scalloped turk's head mold and the other half in a 9-inch layer cake pan. The two layers were then assembled as in the recipe.

Baked Alaska

This classic American dessert is reputed to have been introduced at New York's famous Delmonico's Restaurant in 1876, commemorating the purchase (nine years earlier) of the Alaska territory from the Czar of Russia for the astounding sum of $7.2 million.

Lace-topped Gingerbread is a fanciful name to describe gingerbread as topped with a sifting of confectioners' sugar through a doily, above. On a prized sideboard, right, lace runners underline White Grape Tart with Chocolate Nut Crust, Lace-topped Gingerbread, and Peach Blitz Kuchen.

2 quarts ice cream of choice: strawberry, chocolate, vanilla and/or coffee

½ teaspoon cream of tartar

¼ teaspoon salt

6 egg whites

¾ cup superfine sugar

½ teaspoon vanilla extract

1 9-inch cake layer (basic yellow, sponge, or pound cake)

1. Line a 2-quart bowl with foil or plastic wrap, making sure diameter of bowl does not exceed 9 inches. Pack ice cream into bowl; use one flavor or make layers for flavor appeal. Cover with foil or plastic wrap and freeze until firm, about 4 hours.

2. Preheat oven to 500°.

3. Make meringue: In large bowl, add cream of tartar and salt to egg whites. Using electric mixer, beat until frothy.

4. Gradually add sugar a little at a time, beating at high speed. Add vanilla. Continue to beat at high speed until meringue is stiff and stiff peaks form when beaters are raised.

5. Place cake layer on foil-covered cutting board; put board on baking sheet. Turn out molded ice cream from bowl and place flat side down on top of cake.

6. Cover ice cream and cake with meringue, swirling meringue decoratively into peaks. Cake and ice cream should be thickly coated with meringue. If desired, fit a large pastry bag with star tip, fill with meringue, and pipe decorative designs.

7. Place arrangement in oven and bake 3 to 5 minutes, until meringue turns a delicate gold. Watch it carefully!

8. Place Baked Alaska (on board) on serving plate.

Serve immediately with Brandied Apricot Sauce.

Makes 12 servings.

Brandied Apricot Sauce

Fruit brandies were the rage in Victorian times; apricot brandy lends this sauce its intriguing flavor.

1 cup dried apricots   ½ cup apricot brandy

½ cup sugar

1. Place apricots and 1½ cups water in a saucepan and heat to a boil. Cover, reduce heat, and simmer 15 minutes until apricots are tender.

2. Add sugar and brandy. Stir until sugar dissolves.

3. Puree mixture in blender or food processor until smooth. Serve warm with Baked Alaska.

Makes 3 cups.

FOUR

VICTORIAN NIGHTS

AT NIGHT, THE RICHNESS OF THE VICTORIAN STYLE EMERGES LIKE A FULL-BLOWN CRIMSON ROSE. THE SOCIAL EVENTS PLANNED FOR EVENING HOURS HAVE A DRAMA AND SPLENDOR THAT STATUS-SEEKING PARTICIPANTS DEARLY CRAVED. IF YOU CHOOSE TO RE-CREATE A VICTORIAN DINNER OR BALL, GO ALL OUT IN THE VICTORIAN SPIRIT!

ONE PLANNED ONE'S GARB WELL AHEAD OF THE EVENING, TAKING INTO ACCOUNT THE SPECIAL RE-QUIREMENTS OF DRESS FOR THE OCCASION AS STATED BY SOCIAL ARBITERS. IF YOUR VICTORIAN EVENING ENTERTAINMENT IS TO BE IN PERIOD DRESS, YOU WOULD DO WELL TO RESEARCH WHAT'S APPROPRIATE FOR THE PARTICULAR EVENT.

Balls were very popular among the wealthiest Americans living in cities such as New York, Chicago, and San Francisco, as they provided opportunities to impress each other and foreign dignitaries. To give a ball was to make one's social mark. While William K. Vanderbilt, president of the New York Central Railroad, once said, "Inherited wealth is a real handicap to happiness. It has left me with nothing definite to seek or strive for," his wife, Alva, daughter of Murray Forbes Smith, an Alabama cotton planter, was determined to use her husband's wealth to get to the very top of the social ladder, at least in New York City.

Mrs. Vanderbilt became an energetic, insatiable party giver, and with remarkable success. In 1883 she gave a great costume ball that marked the social arrival of the Vanderbilts at their new home at 660 Fifth Avenue. While the social lions of New York decked themselves out as European royalty in the mode of Mary, Queen of Scots, and Marie Antoinette, Mr. Vanderbilt's sister-in-law Alice Gwynne Vanderbilt outshone them all with her up-to-the-minute costume: the Electric Light.

Follow Mrs. Vanderbilt's example and let your Victorian nights glitter and sparkle, whether you have a sumptuous dinner or a costume ball.

On the gleaming sideboard graced with an exuberant floral arrangement, left, is Roast Leg of Lamb with New Potatoes, Carrots and Red Onions. A sauceboat of gravy, Puree of Parsnips with Orange, and Young Green Beans with Chive Butter are also ready to be served.

THE FORMAL DINNER

"A man who can really give a good dinner has learned a great deal," said Lord Dumbello, with unusual animation. "An immense deal. It is quite an art in itself: one which I, at any rate, by no means despise."
—Anthony Trollope, Framley Parsonage, 1861

An invitation to dinner was the highest social compliment in the Victorian era and one that was not to be extended on whim alone. Members of the middle class were intent on presenting themselves as knowledgeable about social customs and establishing their worth in the community in order to rise within it. Families of great prominence sought to station themselves significantly in the social hierarchy. Therefore, both the middle and the upper classes gave much attention to both the guest list and the menu of the formal dinner party.

Invitations, handwritten or engraved, usually were sent by private messenger to ensure their delivery. Response was to be immediate, also by messenger.

❧

Your Victorian dinner need not be fraught with such social intricacies. Just try to reproduce the delightful civilities of a beautifully set table, wonderful food, and good conversation.

To get in the mood, picture the stately Victorian dining room with its twelve- to thirteen-foot ceiling. It is early evening. The lights are aglow and it is cold. A fire has been laid in the ornate fireplace with its mantel-to-ceiling mirror. The dark oak floor gleams and is almost completely covered with an intricately patterned Oriental rug. The walls have been neatly wainscoted with elaborately patterned wallpapers and friezes above. The light fixtures are chandeliers with several etched glass globes—wall sconces, too, were in vogue. Either candles or electric bulbs are appropriate—the Victorian era encompassed both modes of lighting.

❧

Even if you don't have Oriental rugs, antiques, or William Morris wallpaper, your table can be Victorian. To design a formal Victorian dinner table today, think first of all of opulence and ornamentation. Cover the table with white damask or lace or with a deep jewel-toned cloth—ruby, garnet, amethyst, sapphire, or emerald—with a lace or cutwork runner placed down the center of the table. Use your most ornate china and glassware, adding touches of ribbons and doilies under dishes and between the dessert and the place plate.

Use candles, preferably in tall candelabra, that repeat the color of the cloth. Place one on each side of a tall and impressive floral or fruit centerpiece. Place candles on the sideboard, mantel, and buffet. Use ribbons, posies, and shades to decorate the candelabra.

Napkins should be folded artistically to create visual interest. Inscribe place cards with guests' names and add short lines from Tennyson, Browning, and other Victorian poets. Or, as some Victorian etiquette books prescribed, the hostess may tell the gentlemen guests which lady each is to take in and sit beside.

On a stately dining room sideboard, above, a tiered epergne of American Flint glass, c. 1850, is laden with apples and grapes.

MENU

THE FORMAL DINNER

Claret Punch   Champagne

Cheese Straws   Warm Pâté Tart*

Cream of Watercress Soup*

Cheese Soufflé* with Lobster Sauce*

Roast Leg of Lamb, New Potatoes, Carrots, and Red Onions*

Young Green Beans with Chive Butter

Puree of Parsnips with Orange*

Mixed Garden Greens with Basil Branches

Wedges of Gorgonzola, Mushroom Saga, St. André

Whole-grain French Baguettes

Chocolate Chocolate Intensity* with Raspberry Mint Sauce*

Charlotte Russe with Strawberries

Poached Pears with Vanilla Bean Syrup

Coffee   Tea

*Recipe given

Warm Pâté Tart

A pleasing beginning for a dinner.

9-inch unbaked pie shell

3 4¾-ounce cans liver pâté

¼ cup minced onion

2 cloves garlic, crushed

1 tablespoon brandy

¼ teaspoon nutmeg

2 eggs

1 cup heavy cream

½ teaspoon salt, or to taste

Dash nutmeg

Dash cayenne pepper

1 cup finely grated Swiss cheese

⅓ cup grated Parmesan cheese

Cornichons for garnish, optional

1. Prepare pie shell and refrigerate until ready to use. Preheat oven to 375°.

2. In medium bowl, combine pâté, onion, garlic, brandy, and ¼ teaspoon nutmeg; mix well. Spread evenly over bottom of pie shell.

3. In medium bowl, beat eggs, cream, salt, dash nutmeg, and cayenne with wire whisk or electric mixer until well mixed. Stir in cheeses.

4. Pour egg-cheese mixture over pâté in prepared pie shell; bake 40 to 45 minutes, or until top is golden and firm when lightly pressed with finger.

5. Let cool in pan on rack about 30 minutes. Serve warm, cut into wedges. Garnish with cornichons cut lengthwise.

Makes 6 to 8 appetizer servings.

Warm Pâté Tart on a vintage Victorian goat's foot milking stool is offered, right, along with Cheese Straws and claret.

A selection of desserts have been placed on the sideboard, below: Chocolate Chocolate Intensity, whipped cream and Raspberry Mint Sauce, Charlotte Russe with Strawberries, and Poached Pears with Vanilla Bean Syrup.

Cream of Watercress Soup

In the country, watercress grew abundantly along streams and was used freely by inventive Victorian cooks.

2 medium-sized onions

1 large leek, white part only

1 small stalk celery

1 medium-sized carrot

2 tablespoons sweet butter

2 quarts rich chicken stock

2 cups packed watercress leaves
   and tender stems

2 egg yolks

1 cup heavy cream

Salt and freshly ground white
   pepper, to taste

Snipped fresh tarragon and chervil
   for garnish

1. Chop onions, leek, and celery. Coarsely grate the carrot. In 6-quart Dutch oven or stockpot melt butter, add prepared vegetables, and sauté, stirring, until limp.

2. In separate stockpot or 3-quart saucepan, heat the chicken stock to a boil. Pour over sautéed vegetables and allow to simmer, uncovered, for ½ hour.

3. Add the watercress to the stock and turn off the heat.

4. Puree the soup in a blender, then return it to stockpot. In small bowl, lightly beat egg yolks and stir in the cream. Ladle some of the hot soup into the cream mixture to warm it, then pour back into the soup. Turn the heat back up to a moderate temperature and, stirring, allow the soup to thicken slightly. Do not boil. Season with salt and pepper.

5. Beat soup with wire whisk just before serving. May be served hot or cold, garnished with a sprinkle of fresh tarragon and chervil.

Makes 10 8-ounce servings.

Roast Leg of Lamb, New Potatoes, Carrots, and Red Onions

A hearty dish that can serve as the main course to an elegant dinner.

1 6- to 7-pound leg of lamb	16 small new potatoes
4 cloves garlic, slivered	16 small carrots
3 teaspoons dried or 3 large branches	4 red (Bermuda) onions
fresh rosemary	4 tablespoons flour
1 tablespoon butter	2 cups water or broth
Freshly ground black pepper	½ teaspoon meat extract paste
Salt, to taste	

1. Preheat oven to 325°.

2. Remove the fell (papery membrane) covering the lamb if the butcher has not already done so. With a small sharp knife make slits randomly in the flesh of the lamb and insert garlic slivers and 1 teaspoon dried or 1 branch fresh rosemary. Rub the leg with butter and half of the remaining rosemary and ½ teaspoon pepper.

3. Place meat on rack in open shallow roasting pan. Roast approximately 11 minutes per pound for medium-rare or until the internal temperature registers 140° when tested with a meat thermometer.

4. Scrub new potatoes under running water; leave whole if small or quarter lengthwise if large. Leave carrots whole if small, quarter if large. Cut onions in quarters lengthwise.

5. In large saucepan bring 3 cups water to a boil. Add ¼ teaspoon salt, potatoes, and carrots. Return to a boil, cover, reduce heat, and boil 10 minutes. Drain.

6. Place parboiled potatoes and carrots along with red onions in roasting pan with meat. Baste with pan drippings and sprinkle with remaining rosemary and pepper to taste. Continue cooking vegetables about 30 minutes along with meat, until tender.

7. When meat is done place on warm serving platter. Salt lightly if desired. Spoon vegetables around roast. Keep warm.

8. To make gravy, pour off all but 4 tablespoons of fat from the pan drippings. Add flour to the fat and pan drippings and cook, stirring constantly, until mixture is smooth, loosening any brown particles from the bottom of the pan.

9. Slowly add 2 cups water or broth and cook, stirring, until mixture thickens and comes to a boil. Season to taste with salt, pepper, and meat extract paste. Serve hot in sauceboat with roast.

Makes 2 cups gravy (8 servings).

Cheese Soufflé

In the Victorian era, menus of many courses reigned supreme at formal dinners. Today we scale down the number but find that an eye-catching, appetizing fish course is still most appreciated. This is a do-ahead soufflé.

6 eggs	Dash cayenne pepper
Butter	1¼ cups milk
Grated Parmesan cheese	½ cup grated Gruyère cheese
5 tablespoons butter	½ cup grated Cheddar cheese
6 tablespoons all-purpose flour	1 tablespoon dry sherry
Salt	¼ teaspoon cream of tartar
½ teaspoon dry mustard	Lobster Sauce

1. Separate eggs, placing whites in large bowl of electric mixer and yolks in another large bowl. Butter a 1½-quart straight-sided soufflé dish (7½-inch diameter). Dust lightly with about 1 tablespoon grated Parmesan.

2. Fold a 26-inch-long piece of foil or parchment lengthwise into thirds; lightly butter one side. Wrap around soufflé dish, buttered side against dish, to form a collar extending 2 inches above top; tie securely with string.

3. Melt 5 tablespoons butter in medium saucepan; remove from heat. Add flour, ½ teaspoon salt, mustard, and cayenne, and stir until smooth. Gradually stir in milk.

4. Bring to a boil, stirring constantly. Reduce heat and simmer, stirring, about 1 minute or until mixture becomes very thick and begins to leave bottom and side of pan. Remove from heat.

5. With wire whisk, beat egg yolks; gradually beat in cooked mixture. Add ½ cup Gruyère cheese, the Cheddar cheese, and sherry; beat well.

6. Add ½ teaspoon salt and the cream of tartar to egg whites. With electric mixer at high speed, beat until stiff peaks form. Fold one-third into warm cheese mixture until blended. Carefully fold in remaining egg whites until just combined.

7. Turn mixture into prepared soufflé dish. Refrigerate until ready to bake—no longer than 4 hours. (See note.)

8. About 1 hour before serving, preheat oven to 350°. Bake soufflé about 55 minutes, or until puffed and golden brown. Remove foil or parchment collar and serve soufflé at once with Lobster Sauce.

Makes 6 servings.

Note: If desired, soufflé may be baked at once, without refrigerating, for 40 minutes.

Lobster Sauce

This rich sauce could be served by itself on toast triangles or as an accompaniment to sole or flounder.

1 teaspoon salt	Dash paprika
2 6-ounce frozen lobster tails	1 cup heavy cream
3 tablespoons butter	2 egg yolks, slightly beaten
1½ tablespoons all-purpose flour	3 tablespoons dry sherry

1. In medium saucepan, bring 4 cups water and ½ teaspoon salt to a boil. Add lobster tails; boil gently 5 minutes. Drain.

2. Remove lobster meat from shells and cut into ½-inch pieces; there should be about 1¼ cups. Set aside.

3. Melt butter in medium saucepan. Remove from heat. Stir in flour, remaining ½ teaspoon salt, and paprika. Gradually stir in cream.

4. Bring to a boil over medium heat, stirring until mixture thickens. Cool slightly.

5. Stir a little hot mixture into egg yolks; gradually stir yolks into cream mixture in saucepan.

6. Add sherry and lobster; bring just to a boil. Keep warm.

Makes 2 cups.

Puree of Parsnips with Orange

A marvelous way to serve the steadfast garden parsnip.

2 pounds parsnips	⅔ cup parsnip cooking liquid
2 ½-inch-thick orange slices, seeds removed	Freshly ground white or black pepper, to taste
½ teaspoon salt	1 tablespoon finely shredded
4 tablespoons butter	orange zest for garnish

1. Peel parsnips and cut into ½-inch-thick slices.

2. Place parsnips and orange slices in 3-quart saucepan and add 2 cups water and salt. Bring to a boil over high heat, cover, reduce heat, and cook 10 minutes or until fork tender.

3. With slotted spoon, place half the parsnips and the orange slices in bowl of food processor. Add ⅓ cup parsnip cooking liquid, 2 tablespoons butter, and a few twists of pepper from peppermill. Process until smoothly pureed and pour into bowl. Repeat with remaining parsnips. (recipe continued next page)

The blushing charm of yellow and coral roses commands attention on this mantel, above.

4. To serve, reheat puree gently over low heat, stirring occasionally. Spoon into serving dish; garnish with shreds of orange zest.

Makes 4 cups (8 servings).

Chocolate Chocolate Intensity

The Victorian name aptly describes the intense flavor of this most felicitous dessert.

12 ounces semi-sweet baking chocolate	2 tablespoons sugar
(or 6 ounces unsweetened and 6 ounces	1 tablespoon all-purpose flour
semi-sweet baking chocolate)	Raspberry Mint Sauce
½ cup plus 2 tablespoons butter	1 cup raspberries
4 eggs	Whipped cream

1. Heat chocolate and butter in small bowl or saucepan over hot water, stirring until melted. Remove from heat.

2. Place eggs and sugar in another bowl; place over (not in) simmering water. Beat with wire whisk until mixture begins to thicken and is lukewarm. Remove from heat.

3. Preheat oven to 425°. Line an 8- or 9-inch round cake pan with wax paper and butter the paper.

4. With electric beater, beat warm egg-sugar mixture until light and fluffy. Fold in flour.

5. Fold one-fourth of the egg mixture into chocolate, then fold all chocolate into egg mixture. Pour batter into prepared pan.

6. Bake 15 minutes. Cool on wire rack. Cover with plastic wrap and freeze several hours or overnight.

7. To unmold, dip bottom of pan into hot water about 1 minute, then invert onto platter.

8. To serve, spoon 2 to 3 tablespoons Raspberry Mint Sauce onto plate; top with portion of cake. Scatter a few raspberries around and top with a dollop of whipped cream.

Makes 12 to 16 servings.

Chocolate Chocolate Intensity, below, has a lacy white mantle due to a dusting of confectioners' sugar through a crocheted doily. What a sweet temptation with a cloud of whipped cream and a pool of Raspberry Mint Sauce.

Raspberry Mint Sauce

A very adaptable dessert sauce.

2 10-ounce packages frozen raspberries, thawed

2 tablespoons confectioners' sugar or 2 tablespoons red currant jelly, melted

2 tablespoons white crème de menthe*

1. Use a blender or food processor to puree the raspberries.

2. Add confectioners' sugar or melted currant jelly if raspberries need sweetening.

3. Stir in crème de menthe. Strain through a fine sieve to remove seeds if desired.

Cover and refrigerate.

Makes 3 cups.

*To make plain Raspberry Sauce, omit crème de menthe and add 2 tablespoons kirsch or framboise.

AN OLD-FASHIONED BALL

Mmm, the excitement and fever the invitation to the great cele-
bration ball ignited. . . . I can feel it now and the pulse quickens
still . . .
—So might read a Victorian woman's memoirs of balls
gone by.

A glorious ball straight out of the past, where old-fashioned waltzes, mazurkas, even the polka and the latest "German" (short for German cotillion) are danced, is the stuff from which many a splendid memory is made. Although some Victorians considered dancing foolish or enticing—because of the close physical contact with the opposite sex—balls were and remain a popular social occasion.

The distinction between balls and dances as the Victorians used the terms was that a dance given in a private home, no matter how splendid, was just a dance. *Ball* signified a public function, such as a charity ball or the town assembly. A nineteenth-century ballroom fairly echoes with the strains of the orchestra—a great large-scaled, high-ceilinged room with cream or pale pastel walls. Elaborate plasterwork adorns the ceiling. The polished parquet floors and glistening chandeliers beckon the nimble-footed revelers.

The Victorian ball was the epitome of social standing and elegance. It required the most beautiful, lighthearted, and flirtatious gowns conceivable for the ladies; the gentlemen were attired in graceful well-tailored tie and tails.

Balls were the proper social-climbing Victorian's expression of frivolity and devil-may-care attitude. Dances were more formal in structure but could be fast and compelling nevertheless. Ladies held dance cards that listed the dances in numerical order; partners wrote in their names in sequence.

Flirtations were the order of the hour, and woe to the participant who couldn't cope. Consider the words of a popular song of the period, "After the ball is over, after the break of dawn, many a heart is breaking if you could read them all—after the ball," or this quotation from Tennyson's *Maud* (1855):

All night have the roses heard
The flute, violin and bassoon;
All night has the casement jessamine stirred
To the dancers dancing in tune;
Till a silence fell with a waking bird,
And a hush with the setting moon.

Elegant lighter foods were served, attractive temptations really—heavier fare might impede the dancing and the mood.

The table at a Texas cotillion, left, is laden with tempting desserts. Clockwise from the left: a silver plate holds an Orange Tart, followed by an arrangement of fresh fruit, candied fruit, and bonbons. Next, a gleaming bowl holds Artillery Punch. Other platters hold Filled Ladyfingers, Glazed Fruit Tarts, and other elegant pastries. In the foreground is Cheesecake with Peach Brandy and Fresh Peach Topping.

101

MENU

AN OLD-FASHIONED BALL

Epergne with Elaborate Fresh Fruit and Candied Fruits

Petite Victorian-decorated Chocolate Tartlets

Lemon Curd Barquettes   Filled Ladyfingers

Cheesecake with Peach Brandy and Fresh Peach Topping

Chocolate Truffles

Frozen Nesselrode Pudding*

Orange Tart*

Strawberry Meringues Chantilly

Artillery Punch*

"The Ladies' " Blackberry Shrub*

Café Brulot

*Recipe given

Frozen Nesselrode Pudding

Molded desserts, very popular in Victorian times, tested the skill of the cook.

2 cups light cream

4 large egg yolks

3 tablespoons sugar

1 cup sweetened chestnut puree*

2 tablespoons sweet sherry or rum

½ cup dried currants**

¼ cup raisins**

¼ cup sugar

1 cup heavy cream

Marrons glacés and whipped cream
for garnish

1. Heat light cream until rim of bubbles forms around sides of pan.

2. In bowl, using electric mixer or wire whisk, beat egg yolks with 3 tablespoons sugar until thick. Add scalded cream and stir to blend.

3. Return egg-cream mixture to saucepan and cook, stirring, over low heat until mixture coats a wooden spoon.

4. Remove from heat and stir in chestnut puree and sherry or rum. Pour into container, cover, and freeze until soft frozen. Remove from freezer and beat until slushy.

5. In small saucepan cook currants, raisins, ¼ cup sugar, and ¼ cup water until fruit plumps and syrup thickens, about 10 minutes. Cool.

6. Whip heavy cream until it holds a shape. Fold currants, raisins, cooking syrup, and whipped cream into soft frozen custard.

7. Pour mixture into a charlotte or other decorative mold, cover, and freeze until firm. This will take 6 hours or overnight, depending on freezer.

8. Unmold onto platter. Serve well chilled with a garnish of marrons glacés and whipped cream rosettes.

Makes 8 servings.

*Use canned sweetened chestnut puree.

**Chopped candied fruit may be substituted for all or part of the currants and raisins.

A flirtatious antique Victorian fan with carved ivory, right, also boasts a small vanity mirror on the right.

Orange Tart

An elegant tart for a festive occasion.

Pâte Brisée (follow recipe as in Glazed Fruit Tarts, page 70)

8 medium-sized navel oranges— perfect quality

1 pound cream cheese, softened

2 cups Seville orange marmalade

1 cup crème fraîche or sour cream

¼ cup Grand Marnier

2 tablespoons vanilla sugar*

Mint or lemon leaves for garnish

1. Prepare Pâte Brisée as recipe directs and line two 9- or 10-inch tart pans with pastry. Preheat oven to 425°.

2. Prick pastry with fork, to prevent bubbling up. Cut square of foil larger than tart pan; place in pastry-lined pan. Fill with beans, rice, or pie weights.

3. Bake about 20 minutes, until pastry is golden. Remove from oven; lift out foil and weights. Let tart shell cool.

4. In large bowl using electric mixer, or in bowl of food processor, combine cream cheese, crème fraîche or sour cream, and vanilla sugar. Mix well.

5. Divide cream cheese mixture between the two tart shells, spreading evenly.

6. Peel oranges, cutting off all white rind. Slice oranges in ¼-inch-thick slices. Arrange slightly overlapping in neat circles on top of cheese layer.

7. In small saucepan heat marmalade with Grand Marnier, stirring until melted. Strain.

8. Brush or spoon hot glaze over orange slices, coating surface entirely and allowing glaze to run between slices. Chill.

9. To serve, lift out tart from tart ring and place on serving platter. Garnish plate with mint or lemon leaves if desired.

Makes 2 tarts (16 servings).

*Vanilla Sugar: This is an easy way to have wonderful flavor in all your desserts and sweets. Simply pour granulated sugar into a large jar or cannister and insert several whole vanilla beans into it. Cover tightly. The vanilla will perfume and flavor the sugar in a few days. As beans dry out, use them in cooking, such as in poaching fruits, and replace with moist, fresh beans.

This Orange Tart, above, has been fashioned in a unique scalloped tart pan. The navel orange slices have been quickly blanched, drained, then glazed.

Artillery Punch

A devastating brew, supposedly strong enough to fire a gun.

1 quart rye, bourbon, or blended whiskey	1 cup gin
1 liter dry red wine	1 cup lemon juice
1 quart strong black tea	¼ cup Benedictine
1 pint dark Jamaican rum	Sugar syrup to taste
1 pint orange juice	Lemon peels for garnish
1 cup brandy	

1. Pre-chill all ingredients and put into a chilled punch bowl with a large cake of ice.

2. Stir well, adjust sweetness, and garnish with a few long lemon peels.

Makes about 40 servings.

"The Ladies'" Blackberry Shrub

Blackberries were plentiful in Victorian days and were enjoyed in a variety of ways.

2 quarts cider vinegar	1 pound sugar
4 quarts blackberries	

1. Add the vinegar to the blackberries and let stand 4 days.

2. Strain the berries through a cloth without squeezing, and add the sugar to the juice. Boil in a large non-reactive saucepan for 20 minutes.

3. Cool and serve over ice in a tall glass. (Store remainder covered in refrigerator.)

Makes 2 quarts (about 8 servings).

FIVE

VICTORIAN CELEBRATIONS

*T*N ADDITION TO HOLIDAYS AND FES-
TIVITIES BASED ON THE CHANGING
SEASONS OF THE YEAR, THE VICTORI-
ANS ALSO MARKED THE PHENOMENON
OF "THE SEASON"—THAT IS, THE SOCIAL SEASON. ITS
EXACT OCCURRENCE AND DURATION DIFFERED FROM
TIME TO TIME AND PLACE TO PLACE. IN THE REGENCY
PERIOD, THE LONDON SEASON BEGAN RIGHT AFTER
EASTER AND CONTINUED UNTIL SUMMER DROVE THE
FASHIONABLE WORLD FROM LONDON TO THEIR COUN-
TRY ESTATES OR THE SEASIDE. IN THE AUTUMN THERE
WAS THE LITTLE SEASON, LASTING UNTIL PEOPLE DE-
PARTED TO SPEND CHRISTMAS AT THEIR COUNTRY
ESTATES. BY THE LATTER PART OF THE NINETEENTH
CENTURY THE SEASON RAN FROM MAY TILL AUGUST.

In New York City and Washington, D.C., on the other hand, the Season followed the pattern of England's old Little Season: it began with the National Horse Show in November and lasted till Lent—for the Episcopalians, who included most of the prominent families—and till May for "the rest of mankind."

Along with these social routines was the familiar pattern of the climate seasons—spring, summer, fall, and winter. Despite the urbanization of society in Victorian times, people were still aware of and dependent on the round of the seasons: there was no refrigerated air freight, and no frozen food, so what appeared on the table was still determined, to a considerable degree, by what was in season at the market or growing in one's garden. Then, too, ever since the Romantic Revival of the late eighteenth and early nineteenth centuries, a strong feeling of the superiority of country life over city life, and an appreciation of Nature, figured largely in the cultural milieu. People escaped summer's heat by retreating to the mountains or the seashore.

Another cycle of celebrations derives from the Christian religion, and nowadays even many nonbelievers participate. The history of the celebration and secularization of these festivals is complex, and almost any generalization is inaccurate. With that caveat, we can say that English-speaking Protestants—excluding the Church of England and the Episcopal Church in America, which preserved the Catholic tradition of a liturgical year—frowned on such feasts. They considered them popish, or even heathen—and felt there was not much to choose between the two. It was during the Victorian era that Christmas and Easter began to regain their respectability, and, in the process, to become secularized.

There were also national holidays—in England, Queen Victoria's Birthday (May 25) and Guy Fawkes' Day (November 5); in America, Thanksgiving and the Fourth of July.

❧

The Victorians loved splendor, even grandeur, and they welcomed holidays as opportunities to dress up in the spirit of the occasion, to prepare seasonal foods and decorate their homes appropriately, and to socialize. This was usually with those on their own social level, but in England the country nobility and gentry would sometimes, in imitation or even continuation of older baronial practice, have celebrations for their humble neighbors, tenants, or even servants. Christmas and harvest-time were the most common occasions for these "mixers."

Though some of the standard Victorian occasions for entertaining—Twelfth Night and, in America at least, Boxing Day—are no longer widely observed, we continue to mark the seasons with holidays. On Valentine's Day the Victorian spirit of sentiment, hearts, flowers, and romance can be rekindled with an intimate dinner for two; a celebration of the Christian holy day of Easter can incorporate themes of the coming of spring with pretty blossoms and a meal featuring spring vegetables. An old-fashioned clambake heralds the beginning of the golden summer months; a harvest supper marks the fall social season; and that most typically Victorian of holidays, Christmas, welcomes the winter with the Yuletide feast of good cheer.

VALENTINE'S DAY

The number of letters sent on Valentine's Day, makes several additional sorters necessary at the Post Office in London.
—Robert Nares, <u>Glossary</u>, 1822

The origin of the custom of sending valentines, and the connection with the Christian saint of that name, are shrouded in obscurity. Two or three saints named Valentine—the name is a form of the classical Latin Valentinus, which in turn derives from the adjective *valens,* "strong, powerful, capable"—are mentioned in early martyrologies, but the legends about them are unreliable. At one time it was thought that Saint Valentine might have befriended some young lovers, or that he had written letters on human and divine love; but most modern scholars trace the customs of the day to a medieval belief that birds choose their mates about mid-February. It then became the custom for young people to choose sweethearts—sometimes drawing names by lot—who were called valentines. Notes passed between them also came to be called valentines.

By the eighteenth century the custom of sending valentines to loved ones was well established. At first people made their own, and books were published giving how-to advice or supplying verses to be copied onto them. Edible valentines, in the form of heart-shaped, decorated gingerbread cookies were also popular. In England in 1834, Jonathan King of London had perfected a way of making paper lace. Together with improved methods of color lithography, this ushered in the Golden Age of valentines in the 1840s. (The first commercial valentines in the United States are thought to have been produced by Esther A. Howland in 1840.) The typical Victorian valentine, with its hearts, lace, cupids, roses, and, of course, sentiment, could range from an inexpensive card to an elaborate confection of satin and lace. By the end of the century, however, Momus had triumphed over Cupid, and most valentines were comical—or even lewd. Things got so bad that the Chicago Post Office one year rejected some 25,000 valentines as unfit to be sent through the mail.

A magnificent Tenderloin of Beef Flambé with Burgundy Truffle Sauce, above, reposes on a Gorham silver serving platter garnished with potatoes, asparagus, broccoli, and sautéed zucchini and carrots. The fragrant, rich sauce is in a silver sauceboat.

To the sentimental Victorians, Valentine's Day was a splendid occasion for an entertainment and served as a romantic focus for the hostess's cupid's arrow. Costume balls, at which the guests dressed up as historical or literary characters, were especially favored. A dinner *à deux* might seem more appropriate, but in Victorian times that would have been considered of dubious propriety unless the couple were married.

❧

Nowadays, creating an atmosphere of intimacy is acceptable. Prepare a table for two in a small room, or in a corner of a large one. Choose red or pink, and white lace, for your decorations—perhaps a red moiré or taffeta tablecloth with a lace overskirt. Delicate china with romantic designs of roses, hearts, or flowers definitely captures the mood. Tie a small rosebud to each napkin with a red velvet ribbon. Write a romantic love poem or sentiment on each lace-edged place card. Scatter a few rose petals on the table for a lighthearted, whimsical touch. If you use finger bowls—very Victorian—float rose petals in the water. Place candles on the table, and a cluster of them, of different lengths and in various shades of red, on a coffee table or mantelpiece. A candle in the powder room is another delicate touch. Pour a glass of champagne, and let the rich scent of flowers, the glow of the candlelight, and the beauty of the setting supply an atmosphere of Victorian romance.

MENU

VALENTINE'S DAY DINNER

Baked Camembert en Croûte

Claret Bouillon

Cheese Pastry Hearts

Tenderloin of Beef Flambé* with Burgundy Truffle Sauce*

Pâté-stuffed Mushroom Caps

Potatoes Anna*

Asparagus with Maltaise Sauce*

Mixed Greens Salad à la Russe

Heart-shaped Strawberry Tarts

Frosted Lace Heart Cookies

Linzer Heart Cookies

Floating Heart Ritz* with Raspberry Sauce*

*Recipe given

Tenderloin of Beef Flambé

A festive entrée for a special evening.

5 to 6 pounds (trimmed weight) fillet of
  beef*

4 tablespoons olive oil or softened butter

1 teaspoon freshly ground black pepper

Salt

Watercress or parsley for garnish

¼ cup brandy or cognac

Burgundy Truffle Sauce

1. Remove meat from refrigerator about 1 hour before roasting.

2. Preheat oven to 450°. Fold over the thin narrow end of the fillet and tie with soft cord.

3. Rub fillet well with olive oil or butter. Sprinkle liberally with pepper.

4. Place fillet on oiled rack in a shallow roasting pan. Do not cover.

5. Roast for about 30 to 35 minutes or until the meat has reached an internal temperature of 125°.

6. Remove from oven and sprinkle lightly with salt and additional pepper. Allow to rest a few minutes to settle interior juices.

7. Place on serving platter and garnish with watercress or parsley.

8. Heat brandy or cognac in small saucepan until it appears to quiver. Ignite with lighted match and quickly pour flaming brandy over fillet. Carve by slicing crosswise. Serve with Burgundy Truffle Sauce.

Makes 8 servings.

*Fillets weigh anywhere from 4 to 10 pounds and have a coating of kidney fat on one side and a skin that covers the entire fillet. Have the butcher trim off both fat and skin.

Burgundy Truffle Sauce

A beguiling sauce reminiscent of a true Bordelaise.

2 tablespoons minced onion or shallots

1 carrot, finely chopped

1 tender inner stalk celery, finely
  chopped

1 small bay leaf

¼ teaspoon dried thyme

½ strip bacon, finely chopped

2 tablespoons butter

½ cup burgundy or other dry red
  wine

1½ cups beef broth

¼ cup tomato sauce or juice

2 tablespoons butter

1 cup sliced mushrooms

2 tablespoons all-purpose flour

2 tablespoons chopped truffles

1 teaspoon butter

1. In sauté pan or saucepan, sauté onion or shallots, carrot, celery, bay leaf, thyme, and bacon in 2 tablespoons butter until vegetables are tender.

2. Add burgundy and heat to a boil, stirring to deglaze the pan. Add beef broth and tomato sauce or juice, heat to a boil, reduce heat, and simmer uncovered 5 minutes.

3. Strain, reserving liquid. Discard vegetables.

4. In saucepan heat 2 tablespoons butter and sauté mushrooms about 2 minutes. Add flour and stir well over medium heat for 2 minutes.

5. Add reserved liquid, stirring rapidly over medium heat until sauce thickens and comes to a boil.

6. Add truffles and 1 teaspoon butter. Taste for seasoning. Thin sauce if desired with a little wine or beef broth.

Makes 2 cups.

Potatoes Anna

A potato-loving cook named Anna originated this now classic recipe during the Second Empire of Napoleon III.

½ cup butter, softened

2 pounds Idaho or Russet baking
  potatoes, peeled and thinly sliced

1 teaspoon salt, or to taste

Freshly ground black pepper

1. Preheat oven to 425°. With 3 tablespoons butter, grease an 8-inch skillet with heat-resistant handle or a shallow flameproof baking dish.

2. Layer a third of the potato slices in a circular overlapping spiral around bottom of skillet. Dot with remaining butter. Sprinkle with salt and pepper. Continue layering slices until all potato slices are used.

3. Over high heat, cook potatoes 3 minutes. Then cover and bake in oven 30 minutes. (Place a large sheet of foil or a baking sheet under skillet to catch any runover).

4. Remove cover; bake 5 minutes longer. Let stand 5 minutes to settle; loosen from sides of pan and then invert onto platter.

Makes 6 servings.

Asparagus with Maltaise Sauce

Maltaise Sauce is hollandaise flavored with red juice from the exotic blood oranges of Malta.

ASPARAGUS

2 to 2½ pounds asparagus

Boiling water

1 teaspoon salt, or to taste

¼ cup butter, melted

MALTAISE SAUCE

3 egg yolks

2 tablespoons lemon juice

2 tablespoons boiling water

½ cup butter

Dash salt

Dash hot pepper sauce or cayenne
  pepper

3 tablespoons orange juice*

2 teaspoons grated orange zest

ASPARAGUS

1. Break or cut off tough ends of asparagus, and scrape skin and scales from lower part of stalks with vegetable parer if desired.

2. Pour boiling water into a large skillet to a depth of 1 inch; add salt. Add asparagus with tips all facing in one direction. Return to a boil, cover, and boil 5 to 7 minutes or until fork tender.

3. Drain asparagus well. Arrange in a warm vegetable dish, again with tips pointing in one direction. Pour melted butter over all.

MALTAISE SAUCE

1. In top of flameproof glass or stainless steel double boiler over hot water, place egg yolks and lemon juice. Beat with a wire whisk until mixture begins to thicken.

2. Add boiling water 1 tablespoon at a time, beating as you pour.

3. Melt butter in small skillet or saucepan.

4. Slowly add the hot melted butter to the egg-lemon mixture, beating rapidly with a wire whisk as you pour. Season with salt and hot pepper sauce or cayenne. Continue to beat until sauce is thick.

5. Beat in orange juice, 1 tablespoon at a time. Beat in orange zest. Serve over asparagus.

Makes 4 to 6 servings of asparagus and sauce.

*If possible use the juice from ruby-fleshed blood oranges. Or you may add a drop of red food coloring to give the sauce a rosy blush, but it is not necessary.

Roses are caught in carefree abandon before being arranged in a becoming vase, above. Glistening Heart-shaped Strawberry Tarts, right, hold the eye along with a vintage piano shawl which serves as a tablecloth and an antique vase with crystal pendants.

Floating Heart Ritz

A very lovely romantic dessert as originally served at The Ritz Hotel in Paris, France.

¾ cup sugar	1½ cups heavy cream
3 egg yolks	2 teaspoons vanilla extract
Dash salt	½ teaspoon almond extract
1 cup crumbled almond macaroons	Raspberry Sauce
4 ladyfingers, split*	½ cup heavy cream
2 tablespoons crème de cassis	Chocolate curls for garnish

1. Line a 7-inch (6- to 7-cup) heart-shaped mold with foil.

2. In small saucepan, combine sugar with ⅓ cup water; bring to a boil over medium heat, stirring until sugar is dissolved. Boil gently, without stirring, to 230° on candy thermometer or until a little of the sugar mixture spins a thread when dropped from spoon.

3. Meanwhile, in bowl using electric mixer, beat egg yolks and salt until light. Gradually beat in hot syrup in a thin stream; continue beating until mixture starts to cool, about 2 minutes. Stir in macaroons. Refrigerate 30 minutes.

4. Meanwhile, sprinkle ladyfingers with crème de cassis; set aside. Combine 1½ cups cream with extracts; beat until stiff.

5. Fold whipped cream into macaroon mixture. Turn half of mixture into prepared mold, and cover with ladyfingers; pour in remaining mixture. Cover with plastic wrap and freeze about 4 hours.

6. At serving time beat ½ cup cream until stiff. Unmold frozen heart onto chilled shallow serving dish and remove foil. Decorate top with whipped cream, using a pastry bag with decorating tip if desired. Garnish with chocolate curls. Serve with Raspberry Sauce spooned around base.

Makes 8 to 10 servings.

*If ladyfingers are unavailable, substitute strips of sponge cake or dry pound cake.

Raspberry Sauce

A glistening ruby red sauce.

2 10-ounce packages frozen raspberries,
  thawed

2 tablespoons cornstarch

½ cup currant jelly

2 tablespoons crème de cassis

1. Drain raspberries, reserving liquid. Add enough water to liquid to make 2 cups.

2. In small saucepan, blend liquid with cornstarch. Bring to a boil over medium heat, stirring constantly; boil 5 minutes. Stir in jelly until melted. Remove from heat; add raspberries. Stir in crème de cassis. Refrigerate, covered, until cold. Makes 3 cups.

EASTER

Then comes the brilliant Easter, with its splendid dinners, its weddings, its christenings and caudle parties, its ladies' lunches, its Meadow Brook hunt, its asparagus parties . . .
—M. E. W. Sherwood, *The Art of Entertaining,* 1892

Easter is the major feast of the Christian sacred year, commemorating as it does the central Christian belief of the Resurrection of Christ. Like the Jewish Passover, with which the first Easter coincided, it always occurs in spring in the Northern Hemisphere.

One of the oldest American Easter customs is the Easter egg hunt or egg rolling. Dolley Madison introduced the Washington egg rolling, and when Congress forbade the use of the Capitol grounds for it in the 1870s, President and Mrs. Rutherford B. Hayes (she is better known to social history as "Lemonade Lucy," for her ban on alcohol in any form at White House events) moved it to the White House lawn. The Easter egg is one of those ancient pagan symbols of new life that was early taken over by the Christian Church. The Easter bunny—the notorious fecundity of rabbits and hares makes them obvious symbols of life—is probably of German origin, and was quickly adopted in America. In German neighborhoods one may still see the sweet Easter bread shaped like a rabbit, with a dyed egg tucked under its tail.

Even among non-Christians, Easter continues as a celebration of the new life of spring, as the dormant bulbs burst into bloom and the bare and seemingly dead deciduous trees cover themselves anew with budding leaves and blossoms. Pastels, the tender colors of early spring, are the best tones for an Easter celebration. Floral decorations may include forced branches of apple, pear, and cherry blossoms cut from the orchard, and flowering bulbs such as crocus, daffodils, tulips, and of course Easter lilies. Tie broad ribbons and bows around large vases and pots of these blooms, lace ribbon and bows around the small. Mass pots of Easter lilies together, encircle with a white ribbon, and tie in a large bow.

To decorate the table for a Victorian Easter dinner, place a tall vase of spring blossoms in the center. At each place have small woven silver or rush baskets filled with ivy, small foil-covered chocolate eggs, jelly beans, and sugar cookies shaped like rabbits, ducklings, chicks, hearts, crosses, and lambs.

A traditional main course at Easter is roast spring lamb. In England, however, ham was a favored Easter dish. And in many places the real lamb was supplemented or supplanted by a cake baked in the shape of a lamb. Another seasonal food is hot cross buns. Though possibly of pre-Christian origin, they became Lenten staples during the Middle Ages. And by Victorian times, the fresh, new asparagus—a vegetable known to the ancient Romans—had become the *raison d'être* of spring parties.

An intimate dinner for two, left, begins with Baked Camembert en Croute, Mixed Greens Salad à la Russe, and champagne. The mood is enhanced by the nymph pedestal vase, flickering candles, elegant Gorham silver, and Fitz and Floyd china.

EASTER

Golden Lemon and Pineapple Punch   Milk Punch

Baked Ham with Apricot Glaze

Chilled Steamed Asparagus with Sauce Gribiche*

Baked Noodles with Three Cheeses

Hot Cross Buns*

Eggs in a Nest Salad*

Easter Lamb Cake* with Old-fashioned White Mountain Frosting*

Frozen Ice Cream Decorated Egg Mold

Jelly Beans

Easter Frosted Sugar Cookies*

*Recipe given

Sauce Gribiche

A great cold dressing for chilled cooked vegetables or cold poached fish.

3 hard-cooked eggs

1 teaspoon prepared mustard or ½
   teaspoon dry mustard

½ teaspoon salt

¼ teaspoon freshly ground black pepper

½ cup vinegar, preferably tarragon
   vinegar

1½ cups olive or vegetable oil

3 sweet gherkins

3 stuffed green Spanish olives

1 tablespoon minced parsley

2 teaspoons minced fresh chervil or
   snipped chives

2 teaspoons minced fresh or 1
   teaspoon dried tarragon

1. Chop hard-cooked eggs very fine; set aside.

2. In blender combine mustard, salt, pepper, and vinegar. Add oil gradually while motor is running.

3. Add gherkins, olives, parsley, chervil, and tarragon. Cover and blend just until gherkins and olives are chopped fine, about 30 seconds.

4. Add chopped hard-cooked eggs and blend at low speed 3 seconds. Refrigerate. Sauce will keep up to 1 week.

Makes about 3 cups.

An Easter dinner, left, may include an engaging basket of Eggs in a Nest Salad and Asparagus with Sauce Gribiche. That's a Dedham pottery milk pitcher and Royal Doulton Beatrix Potter figurine, Jemima Puddleduck.

Hot Cross Buns

"One-a-penny, two-a-penny, Hot Cross Buns." What would a traditional Easter be without them?

BUNS

1 cup milk	2 teaspoons grated orange zest
¼ cup butter	2 eggs, beaten
¼ cup sugar	3 to 4 cups all-purpose flour
½ teaspoon salt	1 cup raisins or currants
1 package active dry yeast	½ cup chopped candied pineapple,
1 teaspoon sugar	orange peel, or citron, optional
¼ cup very warm (110 to 115°) water	¼ cup sugar
½ teaspoon ground cinnamon	

FROSTING

1 cup confectioners' sugar	1 tablespoon milk
½ teaspoon vanilla extract	

1. Heat milk until bubbles form around edge of pan. Add butter, ¼ cup sugar, and salt. Cool to lukewarm.

2. Dissolve yeast and 1 teaspoon sugar in the warm water; let stand until foamy, about 5 minutes. Stir in lukewarm milk mixture, then add cinnamon, orange zest, and eggs.

3. Add 3 cups of flour, 1 cup at a time, beating hard after each addition. Mix in raisins or currants and candied fruit. Add enough flour to make a soft dough.

4. Place dough on floured board and knead until satiny and elastic, about 8 minutes. Keep dough soft.

5. Place dough in greased 3-quart bowl, turning to grease top. Cover and set aside in warm place (75 to 80°) to rise until doubled. This will take 1 to 2 hours.

6. Punch down dough with fist, turn out, and knead lightly on floured board.

7. Cut dough in half with knife. Pat out dough to ¾-inch thickness; cut each half into twelve squares.

8. Butter your hands and shape each square into a plump round; place on greased baking pans about ½ inch apart. Let rise until double—45 minutes to 1 hour—and buns are touching.

9. Preheat oven to 375°. Bake buns 15 minutes or until the tops start to brown. Meanwhile, in small saucepan heat ¼ cup sugar and ¼ cup water to a boil, stirring until sugar dissolves.

10. Brush tops of buns quickly with this sugar syrup to glaze them, and return buns to finish baking, another 10 to 15 minutes. Cool.

11. Make decorating frosting: Mix confectioners' sugar, vanilla, and enough milk to make a thick icing. Decorate tops of buns by carefully spooning or piping a ¼-inch-wide cross on top of each bun.

Makes 24 buns.

Note: Although Hot Cross Buns are associated with Christianity, they are filled with pagan symbolism. The cross represented the four quarters of the moon. It was the English who adopted Hot Cross Buns for Good Friday in the early days of the Christian church.

Eggs in a Nest Salad

Spark the children's imagination with this simple salad.

6 hard-cooked eggs in shell (smaller eggs, such as medium or pullet, work well)	Boiling water
	Iceberg, Boston, or leaf lettuce
Red, yellow, blue, and green food coloring (see note)	2 carrots, peeled and cut into thin strips
Cider vinegar or white vinegar	1 cup mayonnaise
	2 tablespoons ketchup

1. Roll eggs on counter or cutting board to crack shells slightly all over.

2. Prepare food colors: In each of six coffee cups or mugs place ¼ teaspoon food coloring. For lavender mix red and blue; for orange mix yellow and red. Add ½ teaspoon vinegar to each cup. Fill cups three-quarters full with boiling water.

3. Place 1 egg in each cup; let stand in colored liquid about ½ hour. Remove from liquid and remove shells.

4. Line a basket with plastic wrap. Shred iceberg lettuce finely to make long shreds and fill basket as if making a nest. If using other lettuce line sides with large leaves and fill center with small leaves. Arrange carrots here and there to simulate twigs. Place eggs in the lettuce.

5. In small bowl blend mayonnaise and ketchup smoothly. Serve as a dressing for the salad.

Makes 3 to 6 servings.

Note: This is a delightful salad for children. If you do not wish to use pure food colors, you can tint the eggs by placing them in red beet juice. Paste food colors were available in Victorian times.

Easter Lamb Cake

Pleasing the children was important in the Victorian era. Sometimes elaborate parties were planned for children to enjoy. This whimsical Lamb Cake served as both a table centerpiece and a fanciful dessert.

½ cup butter or margarine

1 cup sugar

2 eggs

1½ cups all-purpose flour

2 teaspoons baking powder

½ teaspoon salt

½ cup milk

1 teaspoon vanilla extract

Old-fashioned White Mountain
    Frosting

2 cups flaked or shredded coconut

Jelly beans for garnish

1. Preheat oven to 375°. Grease heavily and lightly coat with flour a two-part lamb cake mold. The two halves of the basic lamb mold should hold 7 cups liquid.

2. In large bowl beat butter with electric mixer at medium speed until creamy. Gradually add sugar, creaming until fluffy.

3. Add eggs to creamed mixture and beat at high speed until blended.

4. Combine flour, baking powder, and salt. Add to the butter mixture in thirds, alternating with milk. Stir in vanilla.

5. Place front half of lamb mold on cookie sheet. Fill with cake batter. Top with second half.

6. Bake for 60 to 70 minutes. Remove from oven, allow to cool 5 minutes, and remove top half of pan. Cool 5 minutes longer; loosen cake from bottom pan and remove. Cool completely.

7. Prepare Old-fashioned White Mountain Frosting.

8. Place two dabs of frosting on cake platter. Place lamb cake upright on frosting.

9. Continue frosting, covering cake completely. Coat with coconut. Cut a black jelly bean in half for lamb's eyes. Place one whole jelly bean for mouth.

10. Additional jelly beans and green-tinted coconut* can be placed at base of lamb for garnish. Tie ribbon around lamb's neck, making a bow.

Makes 8 servings.

*To tint coconut: Place 2 tablespoons water and 3 drops green food coloring in pint jar. Add 1½ to 2 cups flaked coconut, cover jar, and shake to mix coloring with coconut.

Old-fashioned White Mountain Frosting

This classic frosting may also be used to fill and frost a 9-inch two-layer cake.

3 egg whites, room temperature   ⅓ cup light corn syrup

⅛ teaspoon salt   1½ teaspoons vanilla extract

¾ cup sugar

1. In large bowl of electric mixer beat egg whites and salt until soft peaks form when beater is raised.

2. Mix sugar, 3 tablespoons water, and corn syrup in a 1½-quart saucepan. Bring mixture to a boil, stirring constantly.

3. Boil without stirring until syrup registers 242° on candy thermometer or until it spins a 6- to 8-inch thread. Remove from heat.

4. Beat egg whites again at high speed. With mixer running, pour hot syrup into egg whites very slowly in a fine stream. Add vanilla. Continue beating just until frosting holds stiff peaks.

At Haderway House, an English Tea Room in Lancaster, Kansas, right, a small pine cabinet holds a Fitz and Floyd teapot and candleholders with an ever-growing rabbit collection.

Easter Frosted Sugar Cookies

Decorated sugar cookies recall happy times of childhood. The Victorian mother cherished her children and planned many treats to please them.

COOKIES

4 cups all-purpose flour	1½ cups sugar
1 teaspoon baking powder	1 egg
½ teaspoon baking soda	½ cup sour cream
½ teaspoon salt	1 teaspoon vanilla extract
½ teaspoon ground nutmeg	1 tablespoon grated lemon zest
1 cup butter or margarine, softened	Colored sugar for decoration

GLAZE

1 cup confectioners' sugar	½ teaspoon vanilla extract
1½ tablespoons milk	

COOKIES

1. Sift flour with baking powder, soda, salt, and nutmeg; set aside.

2. In large bowl of electric mixer, beat butter, sugar, and egg at medium speed until light and fluffy.

3. At low speed, beat in sour cream, vanilla, and lemon zest.

4. Gradually add flour mixture to butter-sugar combination, beating at very low speed. When all flour mixture is added, beat at high speed to combine.

5. Scrape down side of bowl with rubber scraper and form dough into a ball. Wrap in wax paper or foil; refrigerate several hours or overnight.

6. Divide dough into six equal parts. Refrigerate until ready to roll out.

7. Preheat oven to 375°. Lightly grease cookie sheets.

8. On a well-floured surface roll dough, one part at a time, ⅓-inch thick. Cut with cookie cutters using shapes such as rabbits, chickens, hearts, crosses, and flowers.

9. Lift onto cookie sheet, leaving 1 inch between cookies to allow for spreading.

10. Bake for 8 to 10 minutes or until very lightly browned around edges. Let cool 2 to 3 minutes on cookie sheets, then remove to rack with spatula.

11. Frost and decorate with colored sugar or decorations as desired. Or before baking brush tops of cookies with mixture of 1 egg white and 1 tablespoon water. Then sprinkle lightly with granulated sugar. Bake as above.

GLAZE

Combine in small bowl confectioners' sugar, milk, and vanilla extract. Stir with spoon until smooth. Variations: For lemon flavor, omit milk and use 1½ tablespoons lemon juice; for strawberry, omit milk and use 1½ tablespoons strawberry juice.

Makes 4 dozen.

We glimpse a scene in a Victorian parlor at Easter time, left. A basket of Hot Cross Buns, Easter Frosted Sugar Cookies, and a coconut frosted Lamb Cake are ready to be served.

MIDSUMMERNIGHT'S PARTY

And what is so rare as a day in June?
Then, if ever, come perfect days.
—James Russell Lowell,
The Vision of Sir Launfal, 1848

In the age of candles, kerosene lamps, and gaslight, the longest day of the year was occasion for celebration. Longer daylight hours meant evening walks, extended excursions, and above all, the beginning of summer. In Victorian England, Midsummernight was traditionally celebrated on June 24, coinciding with the feast of St. John the Baptist, with huge bonfires that stayed lit throughout the short night. To many Victorians, the perfect days of summer were spent by the sea (suitably attired in suit and tie or bustle and parasol). The Victorian era was a time when seaside resorts flourished; with the improvement of rail transportation, they were more accessible to summer sojourner and day-tripper alike. On America's east coast, summer enclaves of the wealthy, as well as communities of seaside cottages and camp meetings and seaside amusement parks, thrived.

꙳

Gastronomically speaking, the advantage of a stay by the sea was the abundance of fresh seafood. A classic New England seafood feast most popular in Victorian times was the clambake, a simple system of cooking learned, like many practical American traditions, from the Indians. In the late nineteenth century, the shores of New England were studded with clambake resorts such as Rocky Point and Crescent Park in upper Naragansett Bay in Rhode Island. As soon as the weather was seasonable, hordes of vacationers steamed out of Providence and environs by boat to eat the bakes served daily at sites along the shore. That the southern New England clambake truly featured clams is demonstrated by the menu from the Arlington Hotel at Nantasket Beach, Massachusetts, which opens with New England clam chowder and includes baked clams with melted butter dressing and clam fritters. Other items featured include codfish chowder, baked cod, baked bluefish, baked scrod, boiled potatoes, baked sweet potatoes, corn on the cob, and cucumber salad. Our menu includes lobsters from the colder waters of Maine.

Since the Victorian era was the age of steam, it seems only appropriate to have a summer meal that exemplifies the wonderful, succulent effects of steam on shellfish. If you are lucky enough to spend time by the sea, you can construct an elaborate "dug" clambake with the shellfish and corn arranged in layers in a pit. Dig a pit above the high tide mark and line it with large flat stones. Burn wood in the pit until it has turned to coals and the stones are white hot. Very carefully sweep away the fire and place a layer of rockweed, a seaweed that holds moisture, on the stones. Place the cleaned clams on the rockweed, then another layer of rockweed, a layer of potatoes and corn (covered by a layer of husks), then a layer of rockweed and then the lobsters. Blanket the entire bake with a tarp soaked in salt water. Cover it with rockweed and hold it down at the edges with stones to keep in the steam. Keep the canvas moist throughout the cooking. It takes an hour to heat the stones and forty-five minutes for the heated stones to cook the bake.

It's also possible to make a reasonable facsimile of a clambake in a large steamer pot in the kitchen. Either way will produce really delicious eating. Provide plenty of large napkins, cut lemons to clean fingers, and tools for cracking shells and bowls for discarding them.

For a truly grand old-fashioned kickoff to the summer, arrange tables outside or on a veranda and cover with simple white linen cloths. When the shadows lengthen and the short midsummer night begins, light candles in hurricane lamps and hang Chinese paper lanterns. Set the table with heavier porcelain such as ironstone, earthenware, and yellow ware to hold the foods and to serve. Decorate the tables with the roses of high summer or marigolds and zinnias from the garden. To complete the atmosphere of a summer seaside pavilion at the beginning of the season, play period music such as "On the Seashore" (1884) and "Daisy Bell" ("Bicycle Built for Two", 1892).

At the Inn at Fernbrook, Centerville, Massachusetts, right, desserts beckon at the Midsummernight's Party: Tipsy Watermelon, coconut cake and refreshing iced tea.

MENU

MIDSUMMERNIGHT'S PARTY

A Reasonable Facsimile of a Clambake*

New Potatoes with Dill

Corn on the Cob

Creamy Cabbage Cole Slaw*

Coconut Cake   Blueberry Pie

Tipsy Watermelon*

Chilled Beer   White Wine

*Recipe given

A Reasonable Facsimile of a Clambake

This kitchen "clambake" can easily reproduce the basic nostalgic flavor of an authentic stone-dug bake.

1 pound soft-shell steamer clams per person

½ pound littleneck clams per person

¼ cup cornmeal

2 teaspoons salt

1 to 2 boiling potatoes per person

1 sweet potato per person

¼ pound linguiça (Portuguese sausage) per person

1 1¼- to 1½-pound live whole lobster per person

1 ear of corn per person

Dill sprigs

GARNISH

Melted butter

Lemon wedges

Butter

Salt

Pepper

1. Scrub all clams well with a brush under running water. Place clams in a bucket, cover with cold water, and sprinkle a little cornmeal on the surface. Keep in a cool place for a few hours, or refrigerate if holding overnight. The clams will open and cleanse themselves and eat some of the cornmeal.

2. Pour enough water in the bottom of a large steamer or wash boiler to make a depth of 2 inches. Add 2 teaspoons salt. Bring water to a boil, add all potatoes and linguiça, and return to a boil. Cover and cook 15 minutes. Place lobsters on top of potatoes; cover and continue to boil 10 minutes. Place clams, corn, and dill on top of lobsters; cover and continue to boil 7 to 10 minutes, until clams open.

3. Lift out clams with slotted spoon and place in bowl. Lift out corn, lobsters, linguiça, and potatoes with tongs and place on serving platter or individual plates. Ladle out clam broth from steamer into cups for dipping and drinking.

4. Method of eating: Dip steamed clams into clam broth to rinse off any sand, then dip into melted butter and eat. Crack open lobster with nutcracker and cut into bite-sized pieces. Dip each piece into melted butter and eat. You can also sprinkle with a little lemon juice. The potatoes and corn are eaten with butter, salt, and pepper as desired.

Make quantity as desired.

Creamy Cabbage Cole Slaw

Why not cabbage, especially in a zesty slaw?

2-pound head of Savoy or green cabbage	¼ cup honey
2 cups mayonnaise	1½ teaspoons salt, or to taste
2 tablespoons Dijon mustard	½ teaspoon freshly ground black
¼ cup cider vinegar	pepper

1. Remove any coarse, bruised outer leaves from cabbage and discard. Wash cabbage.

2. Quarter cabbage lengthwise. Remove core sections. Using sharp chefs' knife or ½-inch slicing blade of food processor, cut cabbage into ½-inch-thick slices or shreds. Place in 3-quart bowl.

3. In medium bowl using wire whisk, or in bowl of food processor using plastic mixing blade, combine mayonnaise, mustard, vinegar, honey, salt, and pepper.

4. Pour dressing over cabbage and mix thoroughly. May be served immediately, but is best covered and refrigerated and served the next day. Mix again just before serving.

Makes 2 quarts (8 servings).

Tipsy Watermelon

A less-than-temperate summer dessert.

1 large ripe watermelon	1 cup or more light rum, bourbon,
	or champagne

1. Place watermelon on its lengthwise side and cut a deep plug—about 2 inches square and 4 inches deep—into the melon.

2. Lift out plug and reserve. Using a skewer or ice pick, poke holes into the flesh of the melon.

3. Slowly pour in half of the spirit of choice. Replace plug. Tape closed, keeping melon upright.

4. After a few hours, when first dose has soaked into melon, pour in remaining spirit. Refrigerate 24 hours, turning a few times to distribute spirit.

5. To serve, cut across watermelon lengthwise and then cut down melon, making half-moon-shaped slices.

Makes about 30 servings.

AUTUMN EQUINOX PARTY

Come, ye thankful people, come,
Raise the song of harvest home:
All is safely gathered in,
Ere the winter Storms begin.
—Henry Alford,
Come Ye Thankful People, Come, 1844

Though the equal days and nights, the shining harvest moon, and the tang in the air of late September are certainly worthy of celebration, the autumn equinox itself does not appear to have been the occasion of a festival in Europe since pagan times. The harvest-home, or the bringing in of the crops, *was* traditionally celebrated, and though its date would differ from place to place, depending on the climate and the chief crops, a favored date was Michaelmas (the feast of St. Michael the Archangel, September 29) or the nearest Sunday. Michaelmas more or less coincided with the equinox on September 21 or 22, and became a wonderful time to celebrate the harvest and the fruits and vegetables of the season.

Indeed, the American festival of Thanksgiving, though later in the year in November, has obvious connections with the old English harvest-home. English settlers in other parts of America continued to celebrate their harvest festivals in September or October, and looked upon the national Thanksgiving in November as a "Yankee" institution.

In Victorian England, the old land-owning gentry and the newly rich who aspired to join them delighted in maintaining and reviving quaint old English customs. A wagon of grain would be decorated with ribbons and flowers, and the last-gathered sheaf, placed on top, would be worked into the shape of the "corn mother" or "corn maiden." Later, straw pulled from it would be braided and twisted into various shapes—bells, horseshoes, crosses, and human figures—called corn dollies, and hung in the kitchen to ward off evil. A church service—often Evensong—for which the church would be decorated with fruits, vegetables, and sheaves of grain, would be held, and the farmers would present samples of their crops as thank-offerings.

※

For an equinoctial harvest party, the Victorian fondness for featuring one color or a group of related colors in decorations and food is a natural. Choose a burgundy color for your decorations, and a companionable gold for the food. Deck your rooms with symbols of the harvest: sheaves of wheat or corn, pumpkins, red and green apples, varicolored gourds, golden orange squashes, brown nuts, and burgundy grapes and dried corn ears can all echo the beauty of autumn. For flowers choose chrysanthemums (the Victorians loved them) or asters (called Michaelmas daisies in England), along with branches of bittersweet and grapevines. Autumn is also vintage time, so our menu features wine and cider.

MENU

AUTUMN EQUINOX PARTY

Mulled Wine   Chilled Cider   Bourbon Punch

Aged Cheddar with Crackers   Pigs in Caraway Blankets
Cranberry Compote

Cranberry Cornish Hens*

Buttered Poppyseed Noodles   Nutted Wild Rice*

Honey-dilled Yellow Squash and Zucchini*

Spinach Salad with Hot Bacon Dressing

Rye Rolls   Butter

Glazed Apples Stuffed with Prunes*

Port   Brandy

*Recipe given

It's time for an Autumn Equinox Party, above, with Cranberry Cornish Hens, Glazed Apples Stuffed with Prunes, rye rolls, and Nutted Wild Rice.

Cranberry Cornish Hens

A tart and tangy treatment of game hens for an autumnal feast.

4 Cornish hens	2 tablespoons butter
Salt	1 teaspoon salt
Freshly ground black pepper	½ teaspoon freshly ground black
1 cup cranberry relish	pepper

1. Preheat oven to 425°. Wash hens and pat dry with paper towels. Sprinkle insides with salt and pepper. Twist wing tips under birds, pinning the neck skin underneath.

2. In a non-reactive saucepan, combine cranberry relish, butter, salt, and ½ teaspoon pepper. Cook over low to medium heat, stirring occasionally, about 10 minutes or until fully blended and thick.

3. Brush hens with glaze. Place in shallow roasting pan, breast side up, and roast for about 1 hour or until legs move easily. Brush with glaze occasionally during cooking and finish with remaining glaze just before serving.

Makes 4 servings.

Nutted Wild Rice

An easy way to prepare wild rice with the flavorful addition of walnuts and pecans.

1 cup wild rice	¼ cup toasted walnuts, chopped
3 tablespoons butter	¼ cup toasted pecans, chopped
2 cups chicken broth	

1. Place rice, 2 cups water, butter, and bouillon powder in a 2-quart saucepan. Bring to a boil, reduce heat, cover, and simmer about 30 minutes, or until rice is tender and liquid is absorbed. Add salt to taste. Turn into serving bowl and garnish with toasted nuts.

Makes 4 servings.

A bountiful presentation of fall desserts, right, is offered on a silver platter decorated with gourds, squashes, grapes, wheat, and nuts. Shall it be apple pie, cherry pie, or a blueberry nut kuchen?

Honey-dilled Yellow Squash and Zucchini

A sweet and delicious way to serve these late summer and early autumn vegetables.

2 tablespoons butter	½ pound yellow squash
2 tablespoons vegetable oil	½ pound zucchini
⅓ cup honey	¼ cup chopped fresh dill

1. Combine butter, oil, and honey in a large frying pan. Heat over medium heat until mixed.

2. Slice yellow squash and zucchini in ¼- to ½-inch rounds. Add to honey mixture in pan and cook over medium heat about 5 minutes or until tender.

3. Add dill and continue heating for another 2 minutes, stirring occasionally. Makes 4 servings.

Glazed Apples Stuffed with Prunes

A Victorian-style harvest dessert combines cider, apples, and prunes.

1 cup apple cider	½ cup brown sugar
1½ teaspoons granulated sugar	¼ cup honey
8 large pitted prunes	½ cup apple cider
¼ cup butter	4 apples, halved and cored

1. Combine 1 cup cider and sugar in small non-reactive saucepan. Bring to a low simmer and poach prunes 10 minutes. Let prunes cool in liquid. Drain.

2. In small saucepan or skillet, combine butter, brown sugar, honey, and ½ cup cider. Heat over low heat until all ingredients are mixed well. Add prunes and cook over medium heat for 5 minutes or until fully glazed.

3. While glaze and prunes are cooking, prepare apples: Place apple halves, cut side down, on broiler pan and place under broiler, not too close to the heat. Cook for 2 to 3 minutes, until apples are softened but not browned. Turn and cook for another 2 to 3 minutes, until glazed and golden.

4. Place apples cut side up on serving platter. Top each with one prune and a little of the honey–brown sugar glaze.

Makes 8 servings.

A hearty harvest sipper, left, is this Bourbon Punch afloat with cinnamon-spiked orange slices—a fitting refreshment containing bourbon, brandy, apple cider, cranberry juice, and orange juice.

VICTORIAN CHRISTMAS

Before daylight we would wake up to a new world. The whole house had been miraculously bedecked with holly bright with red berries. . . , and a magnificent tree with real *candles stood in the living room, tinsel decked and beautiful . . .*
—John Seymour, <u>The Forgotten Household Crafts,</u> 1987

Christmas is *the* Victorian festival, and whenever we think of the Victorian era, we usually picture it as Christmas time. The feast, of course, goes back much further; ancient peoples, especially in northern Europe, kept a festival about the time of the winter equinox, to celebrate and ensure the return of the sun and the lengthening of the day.

Christmas was especially merry in England, and many of our Yuletide customs come from old English practice—the plum pudding and fruitcake, caroling, the yule log, mistletoe, and evergreens. In earlier times, holly, ivy, bay, and rosemary (which in England's milder clime stays green for most of the year) were the favored greens; but the Christmas tree is the uniquely Victorian gift to Christmas in the English-speaking world. The Christmas tree lighted with candles seems to have originated in Germany, where popular tradition traces it back to Martin Luther. Among the earliest Christmas trees in England were the individual ones that Princess de Lieven, the wife of the Russian ambassador, introduced at Panshanger for the children of her good friend and fellow patroness of Almacks, Emily, Lady Cowper. Then, in 1840 Queen Victoria herself had a tree, to make her beloved Prince Albert feel at home. With this royal endorsement, the custom rapidly caught on. It is recorded that in 1842 a German exile who was teaching at William and Mary introduced the Christmas tree to Williamsburg, Virginia.

In America, Anglicans continued the Christmas customs of England, and Dutch children in New York set out their shoes on December 6 for St. Nicholas to fill—a probable source of our modern Santa Claus. But Christmas celebrations were deplored by the New England Puritans, as they had been by their English ancestors (Scrooge no doubt had a Cromwellian ancestor who, wished a Merry Christmas, said not "Bah, humbug!" but "Fie! Popery"). However, as the early fervor waned and more and more Anglicans settled in the area, Christmas gained ground: it was so merry that in 1793 the chief constable of Boston had to forbid what he called "the Anticks" of Christmas, and in 1856 it was declared a legal holiday in New England.

Christmas cards, too, appear to date from the Victorian era. When or where the custom began is not known, but by the middle of the nineteenth century, handmade ones were widespread, and in the '70s printed cards in various styles were being manufactured.

We should be aware of some important differences between the Victorian Christmas and modern practices. In an age when doing it yourself was more or less a necessity, Christmas preparations began long before the feast—as Mrs. Beeton wrote, ". . . preparing for the creative comforts of those near and dear to us to meet old Christmas with a happy face, a contented mind, and a full larder." The actual celebration took place on Christmas and the following Twelve

Days—not the preceding month and a half, as nowadays. Gifts handmade and store-bought were mostly given by parents to children, and among adults were exchanged between family members, lovers, or close friends. For most of the period, tree trimmings were homemade: paper cornucopias filled with candy, paper garlands, popcorn balls, strings of nuts and cranberries, gilded gingerbread nuts (Mrs. Beeton gives a couple of recipes), and ribbons; glass ornaments did not become widely available until late in the nineteenth century.

※

To give a true Victorian flavor to your decorations, hang garlands of green over doorways and mantels—and over a tall pier mirror if you have one—letting them fall down the sides. Twine greens around the banister or in and out the balusters of a prominent staircase. Hang a kissing bell of greens and mistletoe, with a red ribbon at the bottom to catch the eye, in a strategic spot. In the dining room, festoon the sideboard and chandelier with looping swags of pine or bay or hemlock ropes. Put a pyramid of oranges, pears, and nuts—or some other sumptuous arrangement of fruit—on the sideboard. Robe your table with heavy white damask and place a tall candelabrum, to which red-berried holly has been tied with red velvet ribbon, in the center. Or use an arrangement of red roses. Lay a garland of evergreens down the center of the table and across it at midpoint. Have a small gift, wrapped in white or red paper and tied with a red or green ribbon, at each place. Or get some English Christmas crackers, now available in the United States; these are small paper cylinders that are pulled apart to reveal a toy or other souvenir within, and were very popular in Victorian times.

Looking through the garland-decorated doorway into the living room at Haderway House in Lancaster, Kansas at Christmas time, below. The graceful evergreen garland is adorned with vintage tasseled ecru ornaments, contemporary pink ornaments, and moiré ribbon.

MENU

VICTORIAN CHRISTMAS

Cauliflower and Stilton Bisque*

Petite Parsley-buttered Biscuits

Golden Roast Farm Turkey and Giblet Gravy*

Chestnut and Mushroom Bread Stuffing*

Broccoli with Browned Butter and Slivered Almonds

Mashed Rutabagas and Potatoes

Baked Apples with Mincemeat

Stollen   Pecan Gems

Butter

Cranberry Mousse with Chocolate Fudge Sauce*

Plum Pudding   Hard Sauce

Brandy   Liqueurs

Coffee

*Recipe given

Golden Roast Farm Turkey and Giblet Gravy

The aroma of a roasting turkey conveys the old-fashioned holiday spirit better than anything.

1 ready-to-cook turkey	½ teaspoon freshly ground black
Salt	pepper
½ teaspoon whole black peppercorns	1 tablespoon lemon juice
1 onion stuck with 2 cloves	Stuffing of choice
3 carrots, peeled and halved	4 tablespoons butter, softened
2 stalks celery with leaves	½ cup all-purpose flour
4 sprigs parsley	Worcestershire sauce, optional

1. Remove giblets and neck from turkey and rinse under cold running water. Place in 3-quart saucepan with 2 quarts water, 1 teaspoon salt, whole peppercorns, onion, carrots, celery, and parsley. Heat to a boil, cover, reduce heat, and simmer for 1 hour or until fork tender. Reserve.

2. Preheat oven to 325°. Rinse turkey inside and out with cold water. Pat dry with paper towels. Sprinkle inside of turkey with 1 teaspoon salt, pepper, and lemon juice.

3. Fill cavity under neck skin with about ½ cup stuffing. Fasten skin to bird with skewer or turkey pins. Fill cavity of bird with stuffing; do not pack. Close opening with turkey pins and soft cord or heavy thread.

4. Using soft cord truss bird, securing wings to side of bird and tying legs together. Place turkey, breast side up, on rack in roasting pan. Rub bird all over with soft butter. (This helps in browning.) Place a large sheet of foil loosely over bird.

5. Roast at 325° following this timetable:

Ready-to-cook weight	Hours to roast
6–8 pounds	3–3½ hours
8–12 pounds	3½–4½ hours
12–16 pounds	4½–5½ hours
16–20 pounds	5½–6½ hours
20–24 pounds	6½–7 hours

This schedule is for stuffed turkey; unstuffed will take a little less time. The final test for doneness is to move the leg of the turkey and squeeze the flesh of the thigh. If leg joint moves easily and thigh meat feels soft, turkey is cooked. Also a meat thermometer inserted so that the bulb is in the center of the inner thigh muscle should register 180 to 185° when bird is done. The center of the stuffing should

The tall, 10-foot high Christmas tree at Haderway House, below, is decorated with pink and silver ornaments. It stands in a bay window in the front of the house and at night, with lights aglow, can be seen for miles.

register not less than 165°. Try to plan to finish cooking bird 20 to 30 minutes before serving so that the internal juices have a chance to settle (making carving easier) and there is time to make gravy.

GRAVY

1. Pour off fat from roasting pan. Blend ½ cup drippings with ½ cup flour smoothly in 2-quart saucepan, stirring a minute or two over medium heat. Add 1 quart strained giblet broth all at once and heat to a boil, stirring constantly with wire whisk. Season to taste with salt, pepper, and Worcestershire sauce as desired. Makes 1 roasted turkey and 4 cups gravy. Number of servings depends on size of bird.

Chestnut and Mushroom Bread Stuffing

A variation of the traditional thyme- and sage-seasoned bread stuffing.

2 cups chopped celery and leaves

2 cups chopped onion

½ cup chopped parsley

½ cup butter

2 cups sliced mushrooms

1½ cups chopped, drained, canned unsweetened chestnuts or roasted, peeled, fresh chestnuts

2 quarts small bread cubes, cut from day-old or dry bread

1½ teaspoons dried thyme

3 teaspoons dried sage

1 teaspoon salt, or to taste

¼ teaspoon freshly ground black pepper

Dash cayenne pepper

2 eggs

½ cup chicken broth

½ cup butter, melted, optional

1. In large skillet or sauté pan, sauté celery, onion, and parsley in butter for 5 minutes or until limp. Stir in mushrooms and sauté 3 minutes longer. Add chestnuts.

2. In large bowl combine sautéed mixture with bread cubes, thyme, sage, salt, pepper, and cayenne.

3. Beat eggs lightly, combine with chicken broth, and add to seasoned mixture. Stuffing is now ready to stuff turkey.

4. Or, you may bake stuffing in a greased 2-quart casserole. Pour ½ cup melted butter over top, cover with foil, and bake in 325° oven for about 1 hour. Makes 8 to 10 cups, enough to stuff a 12- to 14-pound turkey.

Cauliflower and Stilton Bisque

Creamy white cauliflower and earthy Stilton make a wonderful soup.

2 cups chopped celery

1 cup chopped onion

¼ cup chopped parsley

1 tablespoon minced garlic

¼ cup butter

5 cups chicken broth

1 head cauliflower (white part only),
   chopped (about 5 cups)

1 teaspoon dried thyme

¼ cup butter

¼ cup all-purpose flour

1 cup heavy cream

2 tablespoons sherry or brandy

Dash cayenne pepper

Dash angostura bitters

¼ cup crumbled Stilton or other
   blue-veined cheese

1 cup heavy cream

Chopped parsley for garnish

1. In 5-quart Dutch oven or stockpot sauté celery, onion, parsley, and garlic in ¼ cup butter until tender, about 5 minutes.

2. Add broth, cauliflower, and thyme. Bring to a boil over high heat. Reduce heat, cover pot, and simmer 10 to 15 minutes or until cauliflower is tender.

3. Puree vegetable mixture and liquid in food processor about 3 cups at a time. Pour pureed mixture into bowl.

4. Heat ¼ cup butter in original Dutch oven until melted. Stir in flour until smooth. Add pureed mixture all at once. Cook over medium heat until mixture boils, stirring constantly with wire whisk.

5. Stir in 1 cup heavy cream, sherry or brandy, cayenne, angostura bitters, and Stilton. Heat, stirring constantly, just to the boiling point.

6. When ready to serve, whip 1 cup cream until stiff. Ladle each serving into soup bowl. Top with a tablespoon of whipped cream and a sprinkle of parsley. (Needless to say, if you wish to forego the last garnish of whipped cream, do so. However, don't forget the sprinkle of parsley!)

Makes 2 quarts (8 servings).

Christmas dinner is served, left: Cauliflower and Stilton Bisque precedes the Golden Roast Farm Turkey, Chestnut and Mushroom Bread Stuffing, and Giblet Gravy. The lavishly garlanded staircase, above, leads to the second floor. The entryway, right, is the setting for the tall family tree.

Cranberry Mousse with Chocolate Fudge Sauce

A light, tart molded creation.

3 cups fresh or frozen cranberries, rinsed

1 cup sugar

1 quart cranberry juice cocktail

3 envelopes unflavored gelatin

⅓ cup kirsch or light rum

1 pint heavy cream, whipped

CHOCOLATE FUDGE SAUCE

8 ounces unsweetened chocolate

⅓ cup boiling water

1 cup dark corn syrup

¼ cup sugar

½ cup heavy cream

2 tablespoons butter

1 teaspoon vanilla extract

1. In medium saucepan combine cranberries, sugar, and 1 cup cranberry juice. Heat to a boil, reduce heat, and simmer, uncovered, 5 minutes.

2. Stir gelatin into 1 cup cranberry juice to soften. Stir softened gelatin mixture into hot cranberry combination. Stir until dissolved. Add remaining cranberry juice and kirsch or rum. Refrigerate until as thick as raw egg white.

3. Fold whipped cream into slightly thickened gelatin mixture. Pour mixture into 2-quart mold. Chill until firm, 4 hours or overnight.

4. Make Chocolate Fudge Sauce: Place chocolate in top of double boiler over (not in) simmering water. Stir until melted.

5. Add ⅓ cup boiling water to chocolate all at once and beat with wire whisk.

6. Add corn syrup and whisk in. Add sugar and stir until blended. Add heavy cream and whisk in until blended.

7. Add butter in pieces to sauce, stirring until melted. Add vanilla.

8. Serve warm with Cranberry Mousse or store in covered jar in refrigerator until needed. To reheat, warm in saucepan over low heat, stirring until liquid and heated through.

9. When ready to serve the mousse, dip mold into lukewarm water for a few seconds, tap to loosen, and invert mousse onto a serving platter. Garnish plate with fresh mint, grape, or scented geranium leaves.

10. Serve each portion of Cranberry Mousse with a little Chocolate Fudge Sauce. Makes 8 to 10 servings.

APPENDIX

RECIPE LIST

SOURCES

ORGANIZATIONS

If you're serious about learning more on the Victorian era, consult with these organizations on their events and publications.

The National Trust for Historic
  Preservation
1785 Massachusetts Avenue, N.W.
Washington, D.C. 20036
(202) 673-4000
Publishes the magazine *Historic Preservation* and holds seminars and conferences. Regional offices in Boston, Charleston, Chicago, Denver, Philadelphia, San Francisco.

The Victorian Society in America
East Washington Square
Philadelphia, PA 19106
(215) 627-4252
Has regional chapters. Sponsors conferences and tours and publishes a newsletter, *The Victorian*.

PUBLICATIONS

Magazines on Victoriana are filled with inspiring articles and pictures; they are great sources for entertaining and decorating ideas.

Victorian Accents Magazine
GCR Publishing Group, Inc.
1700 Broadway
New York, NY 10019
(212) 541-7100

Victorian Homes Magazine
The Renovator's Supply, Inc.
1 Renovator's Old Mill
Millers Falls, MA 01349
(413) 659-2241

Country Victorian Magazine
Harris Publications, Inc.
1115 Broadway
New York, NY 10010
(212) 807-7100

Victoria
Hearst Publications
224 West 57th Street
New York, NY 10019
(212) 649-3700

Victorian Sampler
P.O. Box 344
Mt. Morris, IL 61054-7929
Potpourri of accessories and products for the Victorian-themed home.

SPECIAL EVENTS AND TOURS

Every region of the country has historic Victorian homes. Contact local chambers of commerce, visitors bureaus and historical societies if you're planning a trip to an area known for its Victorian ambiance. Here are a few places in the Northeast worth trying:

The Astor's Beechwood
Bellevue Avenue
Newport, RI 02840
(401) 846-3772
The "summer cottage" of *the* Mrs. Astor with the largest ballroom in Newport. In summer, theatrical re-enactments of 1890s Newport society life. Admission charged.

Historic Hudson Valley
150 White Plains Road
Tarrytown, NY 10591
(914) 631-8200
Tours of historic Hudson Valley homes.

The Mid-Atlantic Center for the Arts
P.O. Box 164
Cape May, NJ 08204
(609) 884-5404
Information on house tours and special Victorian events in the Cape May area.

PLACES TO VISIT

One of the best ways to get in the Victorian spirit is to look at the real thing. Below is a list of museums with period rooms and historic houses open to the public. Call ahead for hours and special events.

Baltimore Museum of Art
Art Museum Drive
Baltimore, MD 21218
(301) 396-7100
Victorian period room, furniture, silver, and Tiffany glass.

Boston Museum of Fine Arts
465 Huntington Avenue
Boston, MA 02115
(617) 267-9300
American decorative arts gallery includes Victorian furnishings. Museum gift catalogue features reproduction Victoriana.

Brooklyn Museum
200 Eastern Parkway
Brooklyn, NY 11238
(718) 638-5000
Four Victorian period rooms.

Chicago Art Institute
Michigan Avenue and Adams Street
Chicago, IL 60603
(312) 443-3600
Victorian furnishings.

Cincinnati Art Museum
Eden Park
Cincinnati, OH 45202
(513) 721-5204
Period room, furniture, ceramics, glass and silver.

Denver Art Museum
100 West 14th Avenue Parkway
Denver, CO 80204
(303) 575-2295
Victorian furniture.

Farnsworth Homestead
21 Elm Street
Rockland, ME 04841
(207) 596-6457
Museum house open to the public June 1 through mid-September.

Grand Rapids Public Museum
54 Jefferson Avenue, S.E.
Grand Rapids, MI 49503
(616) 456-3966
Six Victorian period rooms.

Greenfield Village
20900 Oakwood Boulevard
Dearborn, MI 48121
(313) 271-1620
Living museum with historic houses.

High Museum of Art
1280 Peachtree Street, N.E.
Atlanta, GA 30343
(404) 892-3600
Victorian furniture, ceramics, textiles.

House of Seven Gables
Turner Street
Salem, MA 01970
(508) 744-0991
House built in 1668, made famous by Nathaniel Hawthorne. Five of its rooms are furnished in Victorian style.

Houston Museum of Fine Arts
1001 Bissonet
Houston, TX 77005
(713) 639-7300
Period rooms.

Hudson River Museum
Trevor Park-on-Hudson
511 Warburton Avenue
Yonkers, NY 10701
(914) 963-4550
Four Victorian period rooms.

Louisiana State Museum
751 Chartres Street
New Orleans, LA 70116
(504) 568-6968
Victorian metalwork, glass, and
ceramics.

Lyman Allyn Museum
625 William Street
New London, CT 06320
(203) 443-2545
Victorian glass and ceramics.

Magnolia House
502 North Travis
Cameron, TX 76520
(817) 697-4395
Restored historic house.

Margaret Woodbury Strong Museum
1 Manchester Street
1 Manhattan Square
Rochester, NY 14607
(716) 263-2700
This museum documents life in Victorian America. Large collection of furniture and decorative arts.

Metropolitan Museum of Art
Fifth Avenue at 82nd Street
New York, NY 10028
(212) 535-7710
The American Wing includes period
rooms, glass, silver, and furniture. Mu-
seum gift catalogue carries reproduction
Victoriana.

Meux Home Museum
Corner of Tulane and R Streets
P.O. Box 70
Fresno, CA 93707
(209) 233-8007
Restored Victorian house and museum.

Minneapolis Institute of Arts
2400 Third Avenue South
Minneapolis, MN 55404
(612) 870-3200
Period rooms.

Morgan Library
29 East 36th Street
New York, NY 10016
(212) 685-0610
Frequent exhibitions of Victorian books,
letters and prints. Wonderful gift shop.

Museum of the City of New York
Fifth Avenue at 103rd Street
New York, NY 10029
(212) 534-1672
A wonderful collection of Victorian doll-
houses and toys. Period rooms, furniture, paintings, silver, and porcelains.

Newark Museum
49 Washington Street
Newark, NJ 07101
(201) 596-6550
Victorian furniture and decorative arts.
The Ballantine House, next door, has restored period rooms.

The Peale Museum
Baltimore's Historic Museum
225 Holliday Street
Baltimore, MD 21202
(301) 396-1149
Period interiors.

Philadelphia Museum of Art
26th Street and Benjamin Franklin
    Parkway
Philadelphia, PA 19101
(215) 763-8100
Victorian furniture.

Renwick Gallery
Smithsonian Institution
17th Street and Pennsylvania Avenue,
    N.W.
Washington, DC 20560
(202) 357-1300
This museum of the decorative arts has
Victorian furniture and exhibitions. The
Smithsonian Institution gift catalogue
features reproduction Victoriana and
emphemera published by the Smithsonian Institution Press.

Rhode Island School of Design
Museum of Art
224 Benefit Street
Providence, RI 20903
(401) 331-3511
Period rooms.

San Antonio Museum of Art
200 West Jones Street
San Antonio, TX 78299
(512) 226-5544
Victorian horn furniture.

The Victoria Mansion
Victoria Society of Maine
109 Danforth Street
Portland, ME 04101
(207) 772-4841
Museum house furnished in the High
Victorian style.

Virginia Museum of Fine Arts
Boulevard and Grove Avenues
Richmond, VA 23221
(804) 367-0844
Period rooms and furniture.

Wadsworth Atheneum
600 Main Street
Hartford, CT 06103
(203) 278-2670
Victorian furniture and decorative arts.

BED AND BREAKFASTS

INFORMATION

Bed & Breakfast Reservation Services
World-Wide, Inc.
P.O. Box 14797, Dept. 174
Baton Rouge, LA 70898
(504) 346-1928
(800) 842-1486
This is a trade association. Send $3.00
for association brochure, complete
membership listing.

SELECTED BED AND BREAKFASTS

The Gingerbread Mansion
400 Berding Street
Ferndale, CA 95536
(707) 786-4000
Victorian bed and breakfast.

Grace Place Inn
115 Grace Street
Greenwood, SC 29649
(803) 229-7375
Bed and breakfast; catering service.

The Inn at Fernbrook
481 Main Street
Centerville, MA 02632
(508) 775-4334
Bed and breakfast.

The Mainstay Inn
635 Columbia Avenue
Cape May, NJ 08204
(609) 884-8690
Victorian bed and breakfast.

The Mansion
Route 29 West
Rock City Falls, NY 12863
(518) 885-1607
Bed and breakfast.

TEA SERVICE

Haderway House
100 Broadway
Lancaster, KS 66041
(913) 874-4641
Restored Victorian house; tea service
and guided tours.

FOOD

PHONE OR MAIL ORDER

Afternoon Tea at Rose Tree Cottage
Fine British Imports
824 East California Boulevard
Pasadena, CA 91106
(818) 793-3337
Teatime foods, books, and accessories.
Tea cozies, silver cake and muffin
stands, Christmas pudding, etc. Catalogue $2.00.

Brae Beef
Level 3
Stamford Town Center
100 Greyrock Place
Stamford, CT 06901
(203) 323-4482
Hereford and Angus cattle raised on
feed, without chemical additives. Rib
roast and other special cuts from their
butcher. By phone or by mail.

Burberry's Fine Foods
DeMedici Imports Ltd.
221 West 57th Street
New York, NY 10019
(212) 974-8101
Biscuits, preserves, condiments, marma-
lades, teas.

Crabtree and Evelyn, Ltd.
Peake Brook Road
P.O. Box 167
Woodstock, CT 06281
(203) 928-2766
This is the main branch of the mail order
division; fine toiletries, imported foods,
gift baskets.

Epicurean Fantasys
P.O. Box 1406
Litchfield, CT 06759
(203) 489-1452
(800) 688-7400
Gift packages via mail, including after-
noon teas: English Style, for 6–12 people
with Queen Mother's Torte; Viennese
Style, for 6–12 people includes Almond
Tart with raspberry preserves.

The Harrington Ham Company
Main Street
Richmond, VT 05477
(802) 434-4444
Cob smoked dinner hams, spiral sliced
party hams, ham steaks, breakfast
bacon, country sausage, Canadian
bacon, smoked turkey, smoked salmon,
pheasant, duck, lamb.

SEAFOOD

Caspian Caviars
P.O. Box 876
Highland Mill Mall
Camden, ME 04843
(800) 332-4436
(207) 236-4436
(207) 236-2740 (fax)
Maine seafoods, including: lobster,
oysters, halibut, scallops, North Atlantic
salmon, smoked seafoods, imported and
domestic caviars.

Fishy Business
1000 West Main Street
Centerville, MA 02632
(508) 790-1005
Lobsters, clams, chowder bases. They
will ship clambake fixings nationwide
with one or two day's notice.

EQUIPMENT

Bridge & Co.
214 East 52nd Street
New York, NY 10022
(212) 688-4220
Wide range of cooking items including:
molds, pans, whisks, boards, cutters.
Complete outfitter for serious cooks.

Pantry & Hearth
121 East 35th Street
New York, NY 10016
(212) 532-0535
By appointment. American antique
kitchenware from the Gail Lettick
Collection.

Williams-Sonoma
Mail-Order Department
P.O. Box 7456
San Francisco, CA 94120-7456
(415) 421-4242
Traditional holiday foods, English
Christmas cookies, crystallized ginger,
mincemeat. Willow pattern china, pud-
ding molds, cake pans, lace doilies, fine
cookware. Catalogue available.

BOOKS

Jessica's Biscuit
Box 301
Newtonville, MA 02160
(800) 225-4264
(800) 322-4027 (in MA)
(617) 965-0530 (in Boston area)
(617) 527-0113 (fax)
New cookbooks. Catalogue available.

Kitchen Arts and Letters
1435 Lexington Avenue
New York, NY 10128
(212) 876-5550
Cookbooks.

The Silo
Upland Road
New Milford, CT 06776
(203) 355-0300
Store, gallery and cooking school with a
large selection of cooking and entertainment books.

CATERERS AND CONSULTANTS

Cile Burbridge
12 Stafford Road
Danvers, MA 01923
(508) 774-3514
Maker of elaborate sculptured cakes.

Cheryl Kleinman
32 Downing Street, #3D
New York, NY 10014
(212) 242-6195
Victorian-style cakes, pastry chef. By appointment only.

Cheryl Weatherly Schultz
5206 Vanderbilt Avenue
Dallas, TX 75206
(214) 823-5009
Food consultant and stylist.

The Secret Ingredient
1006 Washington Street
Hoboken, NJ 07030
(201) 656-6446
Caterers and retail shop.

A Sense of Taste
217 East 85th Street, #237
New York, NY 10028
(212) 570-2928
Caterers, by appointment only.

Service Service
1120 West Fry Street
Chicago, IL 60622
(312) 829-4559
Caterers and party planners.

CLOTHING

Amazon Dry Goods
2218 East 11th Street
Davenport, Iowa 52803-3760
(319) 322-6800
Everything for true Victorian living.
General catalogue, $2.00; pattern cata-
logue, $4.00; for first class delivery add
$1.00 for each.

Campbell's Historic Patterns
R.D. 1, Box 1444
Herndon, PA 17830
Patterns, books, antique buttons and ac-
cessories. $4.00 catalogue.

Como-San Clothing
P.O. Box 31141
Seattle, WA 98103
Country Victorian clothing, sun dresses,
nightgowns, morning jackets, camisoles
and bloomers. $1.50 catalogue.

Grannies Heartstrings
P.O. Box 1756
Morgan Hill, CA 95037
(408) 779-3287
Heirloom handmade christening gowns.
$3.00 color brochure.

Lavender Blue
270 Waterman Avenue
Esmond, R.I. 02917
Garden party dresses. $1.00 for bro-
chure and fabric swatches.

Madhatter Press
P.O. Box 7480
Minneapolis, MN 55407
(612) 822-1102
Complete hat making and millinery
book. $20.00 plus $2.00 postage; Minne-
sota residents add $1.20 tax.

Michelle's
P.O. Box 1189
Nashua, NH 03061
Victorian clothing, blouses, etc. $2.00
brochure.

Past Patterns
P.O. Box 7587
Grand Rapids, MI 49510
(616) 245-9456
Historic patterns. $5.00 catalogue.

Poppy
1579 Farmers Lane, Suite 222
Santa Rosa, CA 95405
(707) 538-8919
Poppy's garden picture hat, adult and
children's sizes; $1.00 brochure.

Reflections of the Past
P.O. Box 409026
Bay Village, Ohio 44140
Antique clothing, featuring Victorian
and turn-of-the-century accessories.
$2.00 for 20-page catalogue.

Sweet Material Things
P.O. Box 689
Wall Kill, NY 12589
(914) 687-0518
Vintage designs, including bridal wear,
home accents, toys, clothing.

Victoriana Clothing and Decorating
28 Eby Street North
Kitchener, Ontario N2H
Canada
(519) 744-9430
Wholesale and retail; $4.00 catalogue.

PAPER GOODS

Caspari Greeting Cards
H. George Caspari, Inc.
41 Madison Avenue
New York, NY 10003
(212) 685-9726
Invitations, note paper, tags, gift wrap.

The Gifted Line
John Grossman, Inc.
2656 Bridgeway
Sausalito, CA 94965
(415) 332-4488
Gift wrap, stickers, ribbon, cards, invitations, place cards.

Inger of Sweden
Victorian Scraps
310 East 65th Street, #4D
New York, NY 10021
(212) 737-3531
Victorian scraps; by appointment only.

Merrimack Publishing Corporation
85 Fifth Avenue
New York, NY 10003
(212) 989-5162
Invitations, Christmas tree ornaments,
gift cards, gift wrap.

The Paper Potpourri
P.O. Box 5575
Portland, OR 97228-5575
Victorian paper novelties.

The Prairie Pedler
Route 2B
Lyons, Kansas 67554
(316) 897-6631
Victorian posters and ephemera. $2.50
color catalogue.

B. Shackman & Co., Inc.
85 Fifth Avenue
New York, NY 10003
(212) 989-5162
Large selection of paper goods.

The Winslow Papers, Inc.
231 Lawrenceville Road
Lawrenceville, NJ 08648
(609) 392-1333
Antique greeting cards and tabletop
accessories, sachet envelopes. Free
catalogue.

ANTIQUES

PUBLICATIONS

Antique Review
Box 538
Worthington, OH 43085-9928
(614) 885-9757
Monthly review of auction news, show
dates, dealer and shop locations. Articles
by authorities on collectibles and one-of-
a-kind pieces.

STORES

Newel Art Galleries
425 East 53rd Street
New York, NY 10022
(212) 758-1970
Home of "Fantasy Furniture" plus all
manner of Victorian antiques.

Southampton Antiques
Route 10
Southampton, MA 01073
(413) 527-1022
Meg and Bruce Cummings's collection of
American oak and Victorian furniture.

Eve Stone and Son
125 East 57th Street
New York, NY 10022
(212) 935-3780
18th and 19th century English copper
molds of distinct architectural beauty.

Victorian House
128 North Longwood, Room 201
Rockford, IL 61107
(815) 963-3351
Antique certificates. $1.00 brochure.

SILVER

Basquetrie
810 Rangeline
Columbia, MO 65201
(800) 342-7278
Victorian picnic basket with antique
china, silver, linen and crystal goblets.

Gorevic & Gorevic
635 Madison Avenue
New York, NY 10022
(212) 832-9000
Antique silver.

James II Galleries, Ltd.
15 East 57th Street
New York, NY 10022
(212) 355-7040
Antique silver.

J. Mavec & Co.
52 East 76th Street
New York, NY 10021
(212) 517-8822
Antique silver.

S. J. Shrubsole
104 East 57th Street
New York, NY 10022
(212) 753-8920
Antique silver.

Wakefield-Scearce Galleries
525 Washington
P.O. Box 489
Shelbyville, KY 40065
(502) 633-4382
Antique silver.

TABLEWARE

Fitz & Floyd, Inc.
2055-C Luna Road
Carrollton, TX 75006
(214) 243-4125
Makers of chinaware; retail outlet.

Porcelains by Marilyn
P.O. Box 9074
Burton, MI 48509
(313) 736-7358
Hand-painted porcelains. $2.50 full
color catalogue.

Royal Doulton USA, Inc.
700 Cottontail Lane
Somerset, NJ 08873
(201) 356-7880
Victorian-style china available in Royal
Albert and Old Country Roses patterns.
Beatrix Potter china available in china
plates, tea sets, character jugs, figurines.

Tiffany and Company
727 Fifth Avenue
New York, NY 10022
(212) 755-8000
Elegant crystal, silver, china.

REPLACEMENTS: SILVER AND CHINA

Coinways
136 Cedarhurst Avenue
Cedarhurst, NY 11516
(516) 374-1970
(800) 645-2102
Hundreds of old, new and discontinued
silver patterns. The sterling silver matching service will replace missing pieces or
add to existing place settings.

Haviland Matching Services, Ltd.
3959 North Harcourt Place
Milwaukee, WI 53211
Attn: Grace Graves
(414) 964-9180
Will match china settings.

Noritake China
Service Center
P.O. Box 3240
Chicago, IL 60654
(800) 562-1991
Will find matching pieces for Noritake
china.

Replacements
302 Gallimore Dairy Road
Greensboro, NC 27409
(919) 668-2064
Finds "lost" china; good source of old
porcelain dinner sets.

LINENS AND LACE

Faith's Lacery
89 West Main Street, Suite 103
Dundee, IL 60118
(708) 428-0300
Wide range of laces.

Hattie Fox
P.O. Box 1134
Rochester, MI 48063
(313) 651-4977
Lace curtains, pillows, doilies, table-
cloths, runners. $2.00 catalogue.

Heirloom Ribbon and Lace Pillows
P.O. Box 42
South Laguna, CA 92677
Lace. $1.00 catalogue.

Lace Connection
24 Mill Plain Road
Danbury, CT 06811
(203) 790-1007
Imported lace from Scotland, Germany,
China. Catalogue available.

Laci's
2982 Adeline Street
Berkeley, CA 94703
(415) 843-7178
Fine selection of Victorian era laces,
trims, other textiles.

Linen & Lace
4 Lafayette
Washington, MO 63090
(314) 239-4404
Lace curtains, pillows, tablecloths. $2.00
catalogue.

Linen Lady
885 57th Street
Sacramento, CA 95819
(916) 457-6718
Lace curtains, handmade linens. Wholesale and retail. $2.00 catalogue.

London Lace
167 Newbury Street, 2nd Floor
Boston, MA 02116
(617) 267-3506
Reproductions of Victorian lace.

Orama's
148 Washington Street
Marblehead, MA 01945
(617) 631-0894
Linens.

Rue de France
78 Thames Street
Newport, RI 02840
(401) 846-2084
Imported lace from France.

Victorian House
128 Longwood Street
Rockford, IL 61107
(815) 963-3351
Lace.

Wecker Textiles
P.O. Box 212
Punta Gorda, FL 33950-0212
(813) 637-9225
Lace curtains; wholesale and retail.

VICTORIAN DECOR

FABRICS AND WALLPAPER

American Discount Wallcoverings
1411 Fifth Avenue
Pittsburgh, PA 15219
(800) 777-2737
Wallpapers, borders and fabrics.

Laura Ashley, Ltd.
1300 MacArthur Boulevard
Mahwah, NJ 07430
(800) 367-2000 (mail order)
(800) 847-0202 (decorator collection)
Classic furnishings, fabrics and
wallpaper.

Bradbury & Bradbury Wallpapers
P.O. Box 155
Benicia, CA 94510
(707) 746-1900
Hand-printed Victorian wallpapers, in-
cluding William Morris designs.

J.R. Burrows & Co.
6 Church Street
Boston, MA 02116
(617) 451-1982
Fabrics and lace from the Victorian era.

Scalamandré
950 Third Avenue
New York, NY 10022
(212) 980-3888
Manufacturers of wallpaper, upholstery
and drapery fabric.

WINDOW TREATMENTS

Country Curtains at the Red Lion Inn
Stockbridge, MA 01262
(413) 243-1300
Curtains, lace dust ruffles, valances, fes-
toons. Catalogue available.

Southern Ruffles
P.O. Box 1079
Burgaw, NC 28425
Window treatments.

Vintage Valances
P.O. Box 43326
Cincinnati, OH 45243
(513) 561-8665
Custom-made drapes and valances.

DECORATIVE ACCENTS

Bonne Idee Ribbon
27 Purchase Street
Rye, NY 10580
(914) 967-0370
Ribbon. Decorative ribbons that are
wired to bend and drape. $3.00 for 2
dozen samples.

Dee-Signs, Ltd.
P.O. Box 490
Rusland, PA 18956
A range of stencils including patterns for
wreaths, bouquets, herbs and borders.

FLORAL ACCENTS

POTPOURRIS

Aphrodisia
282 Bleecker Street
New York, NY 10014
(212) 989-6440
Herbs, spices, fixatives and potpourris.

Caprilands Herb Farm
Adelma Grenier Simmons, herbalist
534 Silver Street
Coventry, CT 06238
(203) 742-7244
Flowers, seeds, books, everlastings, herbs.

Caswell-Massey Co., Ltd.
518 Lexington Avenue
New York, NY 10017
(212) 755-2254
Potpourris, sachets, essential oils, dried
flowers, herbs, spices.

Caswell-Massey Co., Ltd.
Catalogue Division
111 Eighth Avenue
New York, NY 10011
(212) 620-0900

Kiehl's
109 Third Avenue
New York, NY 10003
(212) 475-3400
Old-fashioned natural toiletries. Essential oils for potpourri.

Pretty Penny
P.O. Box 23
Orwigsburg, PA 17961
(717) 943-2857
Lace pillows filled with potpourri. $1.50
brochure.

San Francisco Herb Company
250 14th Street
San Francisco, CA 94103
(800) 227-4530
(800) 622-0768 (in CA)
Recipes, ingredients, fragrance oils and
spices for potpourris. Free catalogue.

Varney's Chemist-Laden
242 West Main Street
Fredericksburg, TX 78624
(512) 997-8615
(800) 284-0526
A fine fragrance, toiletries, and herb
shop. Also tussy mussies, essential oils,
ingredients for potpourri, and more.

Victorian Potpourri
384 Case Road
Lakewood, NJ 08701
(800) 344-0070
Victorian potpourri by the pound.

EVERLASTINGS

Clarisa Benlolo
1441 Southwest 19th Street
Boca Raton, FL 33486
Dried flowers, baskets, wreaths and
straw hats for everlastings. $1.00
brochure.

Everlasting Designs
P.O. Box 129
Yorkville, NY 13495
Dried flower topiaries, wreaths and bas-
kets. $1.00 brochure.

Floradora
R.D. #1, Box 1092
Stroudsburg, PA 18360
(717) 476-1935
Roses and seasonal blooms for the Victo-
rian bride. Brochure.

FLORAL ARRANGEMENTS

M. M. Fenner Company
73 Leonard Street
New York, NY 10013
(212) 219-0099
Floral arrangements for celebrations.

Llewellyn & Madelyn
Floral Decorators
Aldrich Terrace
Marblehead, MA 01945
(617) 631-4598
Floral arrangements.

Victorian Visions
22 Worcester Avenue
Turners Falls, MA 01376
(413) 863-2461
Custom bouquets, hairpieces, place
cards; by appointment.

ACCESSORIES FOR THE HOME

STORES AND CATALOGUES

The Band Box
P.O. Box 73
Wyoming, RI 02898
(401) 539-7728
Unique designs in decorative accessories, with an accent on French and Victorian elegance.

The Bombay Company
P.O. Box 161009
Fort Worth, TX 76161-1009
(817) 870-1847
18th and 19th century antique reproductions of home decorations.

Elizabeth Bradley Designs, Ltd.
1 West End, Beaumaris
Anglesey, N. Wales
Great Britain LL58 8BD
(0248) 811055
Victorian needlework kits. Printed patterns, canvas, yarns, instructions.

The Carpetbagger
Maddock Hill Road
Madison, NH 03849
Victorian accessories for the home in
silks and satins. $2.00 brochure.

Chanaberry's
421 West Benson Avenue
Willmar, MN 56201
(612) 231-2766
Victorian giftware and home decor.

Gerlachs of Lech
P.O. Box 213
Emmaus, PA 18049
(215) 965-9181
Victorian Christmas ornaments,
decorations.

Heath Sedgwick
P.O. Box 1305
Stony Brook, NY 11790
(516) 589-3633
Elegant Victorian home accessories.
$3.00 catalogue.

Lynn Hollyn Associates, Inc.
853 Broadway
New York, NY 10003
(212) 505-8592
Wallcoverings, fabrics, china, notepaper, gift wrap, cards, and furniture.

Hudson Street Papers
234 Third Avenue
New York, NY 10013
(212) 529-9748
Victorian-inspired invitations, cards,
notepaper, gift wrap, china, books, accessories and lamps.

Land Called Camelot
3842 Gladeridge Drive
Houston, TX 77068
Victorian accessories in porcelain and
lace. $2.00 color brochure.

Sandra Lawrence
4135 Fariss Lane
Elsobrante, CA 94803
Victorian fans.

Lexington Gardens
1008 Lexington Avenue
New York, NY 10021
(212) 861-4390
Garden and home accessories including
wire bird cages, stationery, picture
frames, placemats, napkins and sconces.

Nicole's Cottage
579 New Leicester Highway
Asheville, NC 28806
(704) 253-9567
French Victorian romance collection.

Pieces of Olde
P.O. Box 65130
716 West 36th Street
Baltimore, MD 21209
(301) 366-4949
Dolls and accessories, patterns and kits.
$2.00 catalogue.

Rose & Gerard
55 Sunnyside
Mill Valley, CA 94941
(415) 383-4050
Majolica, Victorian tin plates, cast-iron
and wicker garden furniture, potpourri.

Sweet Nellie
1262 Madison Avenue
New York, NY 10128
(212) 876-5775
Quilts, pillows, picture frames, candles,
china, afghans, coverlets.

Wolfman Gold & Good Co.
116 Greene Street
New York, NY 10013
(212) 431-1888
China, placemats, napkins, glassware,
lace, pillows, linens.

PICTURE FRAMES

English Silver Frames by Mara
P.O. Box 4442
Marietta, GA 30061
(404) 427-4798
Frames and silver gifts. $3.00 catalogue.

Exposures
9180 Le Saint Drive
Fairfield, Ohio 45014
(513) 874-9600
(800) 222-4947
Victorian-style pewter frames and photo
albums. Photo copy and restoration.
$2.00 catalogue.

i was framed
1577 West 132nd Street
Gardena, CA 90249
(213) 327-6265
Fabric-covered frames and storage accessories for the home.

Museum Memories
1433-H West Fullerton Avenue
Addison, IL 60101
(312) 628-2288
Reproductions and picture frames in
small, personal sizes. $2.00 color catalog.

Old Tyme Picture Frames
P.O. Box 4791
Downey, CA 90241
(213) 803-1236
Picture frames. $1.00 catalogue.

SIGNS

English Country Signs
24 Phoenixville Pike
Malvern, PA 19355
(215) 296-2839
(215) 640-5896 (fax)
Assorted signs.

Expressions in Wood
961 East New Lenox Road
Lenox, MA 01240
(413) 637-1662
Hand-carved signs to adorn the home.
Custom-carved items available.

REPRODUCTION FIXTURES AND FURNITURE

STORES AND CATALOGUES

Ballard Designs
2148-J Hills Avenue
Atlanta, GA 30318
(404) 351-5099
Architectural accents for the home and garden. Catalogue available.

Crawford's Old House Store
550 Elizabeth Street
Waukesha, WI 43186
(800) 556-7878
Victorian general store with lighting, plumbing, stencil kits, moldings, and fireplace mantels.

Victorian Warehouse
190 Grace Street
Auburn, CA 95603
(916) 823-0374
Elegant home items, including gazebos, beveled glass doors, ceiling and lighting fixtures, bathroom accessories, curtains, lampshades. $3.00 catalogue.

LIGHTS AND LAMPSHADES

Thomas Industries, Inc.
950 Breckenridge Lane
Louisville, KY 40207
(502) 894-2400
Reproduction fixtures, chandeliers, sconces, bath strips, decorative electrical products.

Victorian Lightcrafters, Ltd.
P.O. Box 350
Slate Hill, NY 10973
(914) 355-1300
Assorted light fixtures.

Burdoch Victorian Lamp Co.
1145 Industrial Avenue, #E-2
Escondido, CA 92025
(619) 745-3275
Lampshades. $5.00 brochure.

Sue Johnson
1745 Solano Avenue
Berkeley, CA 94707
(415) 527-2623
Handmade and embroidered lampshades.

Roy Electric Co., Inc.
1054 Coney Island Avenue
Brooklyn, NY 11230
(718) 434-7002
Lighting catalogue $4.00. Also antique brass showers and fixtures. Plumbing catalogue $5.00.

Shades of a New Dawn
621 Fourth Street
Clovis, CA 93612
(209) 297-1514
Supplies for making your own silk lampshades.

Shades of the Past
P.O. Box 502
Corte Madera, CA 94925
(415) 459-6999
Hand-sewn Victorian silk lampshades; also restoration work.

HARDWARE

Besco Plumbing
729 Atlantic Avenue
Boston, MA 02111
(617) 423-4535
Assorted antique-style plumbing including shower systems, tubs, sinks, and accessories.

Hinges and Handles
100 Lincolnway East
Osceloa, IN 46561
(800) 533-4782
Reproductions of classic porcelain door-knobs and door hardware.

FURNITURE

D & S Woodworks
P.O. Box 2236
Ventura, CA 93001
(805) 652-0292
Vintage folding screens. $1.00 brochure.

Heirloom Fine Furnishings
3621 McGehee Road
Montgomery, AL 36111
(800) 288-1513
Furniture reproductions. $2.00 catalogue.

Wesley Allen, Inc.
10001 East 60th Street
Los Angeles, CA 90001
(213) 231-0619
(800) 541-3027
Reproduction beds.

Woodcreek Furniture
P.O. Box 621107
Littleton, CO 80162
Reproduction furniture including oak ice box, coffee tables. $2.50 catalogue.

GARDEN ACCESSORIES

Architectural Originals
P.O. Box 8023
Newport Beach, CA 92658
(714) 559-4961
Victorian gothic birdhouse.

Gardener's Eden
Williams-Sonoma
P.O. Box 7307
San Francisco, CA 94120-7307
(415) 421-4242
Gardening supplies; call for catalogue.

La Jolla Sales Co.
6910 Dennison Street
San Diego, CA 92122
(619) 452-2044
Reproduction cast-aluminum garden furniture. $2.00 catalogue.

Moultrie Manufacturing Co.
Box 1179
Moultrie, GA 31776-1179
(800) 841-8674
Victorian cast-aluminum and cast-iron furniture; $3.00 color catalogue.

Smith & Hawken
35 Corte Madera Avenue
Mill Valley, CA 94941
(415) 381-1800
Garden furniture and supplies; mail-order.

White Swan
8104 S.W. Nimbus Avenue
Beaverton, OR 97005
(503) 641-4477
(800) 233-7926
Garden accents in solid bronze, sun dials, decorative accessories, weather-vanes, birdbaths.

BIBLIOGRAPHY

CULINARY BOOKS

The American Heritage Cookbook and Illustrated History of American Eating & Drinking. By the Editors of *American Heritage.* New York: American Heritage Publishing Co., Inc., 1964.

Bailey, Adrian. *Foods of the World: The Cooking of the British Isles.* New York: Time-Life Books Inc., 1969.

Beard, James A. *James Beard's American Cookery.* Boston: Little, Brown and Company, 1972.

Beeton, Mrs. Isabella. *Mrs. Beeton's English Cookery with 2,000 practical recipes.* Reprint. New York: Crown Publishers, Inc., 1952.

Berger, Frances de Talavera and John Parke Custis. *Sumptuous Dining in Gaslight San Francisco.* New York: Doubelday & Co., 1985.

Better Homes and Gardens Heritage Cookbook: The Story of Food in American Life. Des Moines: Meredith Corporation, 1975.

Black, Naomi. *Seashore Entertaining.* Philadelphia: Running Press, 1987.

Cannon, Poppy and Patricia Brooks. *The President's Cookbook: Practical Recipes from George Washington to the Present.* Ramsey, NJ: Funk & Wagnalls, 1968.

The Fannie Farmer Cookbook, 11th edition. Revised by Wilma Lord Perkins. Boston: Little, Brown and Company, 1965.

Fobel, Jim. *Jim Fobel's Old Fashioned Baking Book: Recipes from an American Childhood.* New York: Ballantine Books, 1987.

Foley, Tricia. *Tea: Recipes & Table Settings.* New York: Clarkson N. Potter, 1987.

Grover, Kathryn, ed. *Dining in America 1850–1900.* Amherst, MA: The University of Massachusetts Press, 1987.

Henderson, Mary F. *Practical Cooking and Dinner Giving.* New York: Harper, 1876.

Hess, John L. and Karen Hess. *The Taste of America.* New York: Grossman Publishers, 1977.

Hildene Hospitality: Then and Now. Manchester, VT: Friends of Hildene, Inc., 1982.

Jones, Evan. *American Food: The Gastronomic Story.* New York: Vintage Books, 1981.

King, Caroline B. *Victorian Cakes: A Reminiscence with Recipes.* Berkeley: AMS Books/Harris Publishing Co., Inc., 1986.

Leslie, Eliza. *Seventy-Five Receipts for Pastry, Cakes and Sweetmeats, by a Lady of Philadelphia.* Boston: Monroe and Francis, 1828. Reprint. Cambridge, MA: Applewood Books, 1988.

———. *New Receipts for Cooking.* Philadelphia: Peterson Publishing, 1854.

Root, Waverly and Richard de Rochemont. *Eating in America: A History.* New York: Ecco Press, 1976.

Rorer, Sarah Tyson. *Philadelphia Cook Book: A Manual of Home Economies.* Philadelphia: Arnold Publishers, 1886.

Ross, Ishbel. *Taste in America.* New York: Thomas Y. Crowell, 1967.

Sass, Lorna J. *Christmas Feasts.* New York: The Metropolitan Museum of Art, 1981.

Simpson, Helen. *The Ritz Book of Afternoon Tea.* New York: Arbor House, 1988.

———. *The Ritz Book of English Breakfasts.* New York: Arbor House, 1988.

Tannahill, Reay. *Food In History.* New York: Stein & Day Publishers, 1973.

Trager, James. *The Foodbook.* New York: Grossman Publishers, Inc., 1970.

Williams, Susan. *Savory Suppers and Fashionable Feasts: Dining in Victorian America.* New York: Pantheon, 1985.

Ziemann, Hugo and Mrs. F. L. Gillette. *The White House Cook Book.* 1903 edition, first published in 1887. Reprint. Old Greenwich, CT: Devin-Adair Publishers, 1983.

ENTERTAINING AND SOCIAL HISTORY

Auchincloss, Louis. *The Vanderbilt Era: Profiles of a Gilded Age.* New York: Charles Scribner's Sons, 1989.

Beecher, Catharine E. and Harriet Beecher Stowe. *The American Woman's Home.* New York: J.B. Ford, 1869.

Beeton, Isabella, *The Book of Household Management.* London: 1861. Reprint. New York: Farrar, Straus & Giroux, 1968.

Charlton, James and Barbara Gilson, eds. *A Christmas Feast: A Treasury of Yuletide Stories and Poems for the Whole Family.* New York: Nelson Doubleday, Inc., 1976.

Child, Mrs. *The American Frugal Housewife: Dedicated to those who are not ashamed of economy.* Boston: Carter Hendee & Co., 1833. Reprint. Boston: Applewood Books, 1986.

Day, Charles Wilson. *The American Ladies and Gentlemen's Manual of Elegance, Fashion, and True Politeness.* 1849.

Freeman, John Crosby. *Victorian Entertaining.* Philadelphia: Running Press, 1989.

Gentry, Patricia. *Teatime Celebrations.* San Francisco: 101 Productions, 1988.

Girouard, Mark. *Life in the English Country House.* New Haven: Yale University Press, 1978.

Green, Harvey with Mary Ellen Perry. *The Light of the Home: An Intimate View of the Lives of Women in Victorian America.* New York: Pantheon Books, 1983.

Hart, Cynthia and John Grossman, text by Priscilla Dunhill. *A Victorian Scrapbook: Forget-Me-Nots From the Victorian Era*. New York: Workman Publishing Company, Inc., 1989.

Holland, Bettie. "Victoriana Part II." *The Mid-Atlantic Antiques Magazine,* August, 1989.

Hughes, M.V. *A Victorian Family 1870–1900*. New York: Oxford University Press, 1946.

Lasdun, Susan. *Victorians at Home.* New York: Viking, 1981.

Leslie, Eliza. *The Behaviour Book: A Manual for Ladies.* 1853.

Lever, Tresham, ed. *The Letters of Lady Palmerston.* London. Transatlantic Arts, Inc., 1957.

Lipsett, Linda Otto. *To Love and To Cherish: Brides Remembered.* San Francisco: The Quilt Digest Press, 1989.

Manners: A Handbook of Social Customs. New York: 1883.

McAllister, Ward. *Society As I Have Found It.* New York: Cassell, 1890.

Pickles, Sheila, ed. *A Victorian Posy.* New York: Harmony Books, 1987.

Reaske, Christopher R. *Croquet: The Gentle but Wicket Game.* New York: E.P. Dutton, 1988.

Roberts, Robert. *Roberts' Guide for Butlers and Other Household Staff.* 1827. Reprint, Chester, CT: Applewood Books/Globe Pequot Press, 1988.

Ross, Pat. *The Pleasure of Your Company: The Sweet Nellie Book of Traditional Sentiments and Customs of Proper Entertaining.* New York: Viking Studio Books, 1989.

———. *With Thanks and Appreciation: The Sweet Nellie Book of Thoughts, Sentiments, Tokens and Traditions of the Past.* New York: Viking Studio Books, 1989.

Sernaques, Vivienne. *Classic Children's Games.* New York: Dell Publishing, 1988.

Seymour, John. *The Forgotten Household Crafts.* New York: Alfred A. Knopf, 1987.

Sherwood, M.E.W. *The Art of Entertaining.* New York: Dodd, Mead & Co., 1892.

Stowe, Harriet Beecher. *Pink and White Tyranny: A Society Novel.* Boston: Roberts Brothers, 1871. Reprint, with introduction by Judith Martin. New York: New American Library, 1988.

Strong, L.A.G. *English Domestic Life During the Last 200 Years.* London: George Allen and Unwin, 1950.

Topper, Hans and Helena York. *Napkin Folding and Place Cards for Festive Tables.* Translated by Elizabeth Reinersmann. New York: Sterling Publishing, 1989.

Van Gelder, Lindsey and Jerry E. Patterson. "Forever Fifth." *Town and Country,* September 1989.

CLOTHING, FURNITURE AND DECOR

Bishop, Robert and Patricia Coblentz. *The World of Antiques, Art, and Architecture in Victorian America.* New York: E.P. Dutton, 1979.

Coleman, Elizabeth Ann. *The Opulent Era: Fashions of Worth, Doncet and Pingat.* Brooklyn: The Brooklyn Museum, 1989.

Enders, Alexandra. "Setting Standards." *Art and Antiques,* December 1989.

Fairbanks, Jonathan L. and Elizabeth Bidwell Bates. *American Furniture 1620 to the Present.* New York: Richard Marek Publishers, Inc., 1981.

Grier, Katherine C. *Culture and Comfort: People, Parlors and Upholstery 1850–1930.* Amherst, MA: University of Massachusetts Press, 1988.

Leopold, Allison Kyle. *Victorian Splendor: Re-Creating America's 19th-Century Interiors.* New York: Stewart, Tabori and Chang, 1986.

Levin, Betty Bergman with Patricia O'Connell. *A re-creation of Victorian Secrets, An Authentic Reproduction for the Boudoir and Bath.* A facsimile of four chapters of *Our Deportment, or the Manners, Conduct and Dress of The Most Refined Society* by John H. Young A. M. W.C. King & Co., 1883. Reprint. Newton Center, MA: Sources Publication, 1987.

Lichten, Frances. *Decorative Art of Victoria's Era.* New York: Charles Scribner's Sons, 1950.

Loring, John. *Tiffany's 150 Years.* New York: Doubleday & Co., 1987.

Newman, Bruce. *Fantasy Furniture.* New York: Rizzoli, 1989.

Tozer, Jane and Sarah Levitt. *Fabric of Society: A Century of People and Their Clothes 1770–1870.* Manchester, England: Laura Ashley Ltd., 1983.

Warwick, Kathleen and Shirley Nilsson. *Legacy of Lace: Identifying, Collecting and Preserving American Lace.* New York: Crown Publishers, 1988.

Wissinger, Joanna. *Victorian Details: Enhancing Antique and Contemporary Homes with Period Accents.* New York: E.P. Dutton, 1990.

FLOWERS AND GARDENS

Cowles, Fleur. *Flower Decorations.* New York: Villard, 1985.

Stuart, David. *The Garden Triumphant: A Victorian Legacy.* New York: Harper & Row, Publishers, 1988.

Swarthout, Doris L. *An Age of Flowers: Nature, Sense and Sentiment in Victorian America.* Old Greenwich, CT: Chatham Press, 1975.

Tolley, Emelie and Chris Mead. *Herbs: Gardens, Decorations, and Recipes.* New York: Clarkson N. Potter, Inc., 1985.

Verey, Rosemary. *The Flower Arranger's Garden.* London: Conran Octopus, 1989.

PHOTO CREDITS

Page numbers refer to illustrations

Ron Anderson for Haderway House, *7(bottom), 60–61, 61, 107, 123, 138, 140, 142(2), 143, 144;* Keith Conklin for Fitz & Floyd, *17, 27(2), 31, 70, 82, 85, 86, 87, 100, 103, 104, 110, 115, 116;* Franklin Photography, *46(bottom), 64, 73;* Tony Giammarino, *6(2), 10(bottom), 16, 19, 24, 25, 26, 29, 30, 33(top), 45, 46(top), 53, 54, 57, 81, 88, 89, 90, 91, 93, 94, 99, 119, 125, 127, 128, 133, 135, 136;* Michael Grand, *14–15;* Melanie Heinrich, *10(top), 11, 12, 13;* Balthazar Korab, *18, 36;* Dennis Krukowski, *2, 33(bottom), 34–35, 35, 42, 62, 67, 69, 75, 76, 79;* Maker's Mark, *15;* Kent Oppenheimer, *22, 106;* Victor Schrager for M.M. Fenner Company, *20, 23, 27(2), 84, 97, 114;* Brian Vanden Brink, *8–9;* Joan Hix Vanderschuit, *9, 21;* Peter Woloszynski, *32;* Dan Zaitz for Service Service, *7(top), 38, 40, 49, 51(2), 52.*

CREDITS

Page numbers refer to illustrations

FOOD

The Inn at Fernbrook: *45, 46, 127, 128*
Grace Place Inn: *46, 64, 73*
Haderway House: *60, 61, 107, 123, 138, 140, 142, 143, 144*
Margi Hemingway: *88, 89, 90, 93, 94, 99*
The Mansion: *34, 35, 42, 75, 76, 79*
The Secret Ingredient: *133, 135, 136*
Cile Burbidge: *81*
Cheryl Weatherly Schultz: *17, 27, 31, 70, 82, 85, 86, 100, 104, 110, 115, 116*
Service Service: *38, 40, 49, 51(2), 52*

FLOWER ARRANGEMENTS AND ACCESSORIES

The Basquetrie: *75, 76, 79*
Fitz & Floyd: *17, 27(2), 31, 70, 82, 85, 86, 87, 100, 103, 104, 110, 115, 116*
Hudson Street Papers: *16, 26, 119, 125*
M.M. Fenner Company: *20, 23, 27(2), 84, 97, 114*
Smith & Hemingway Associates: *24, 29, 88, 89, 90, 91, 93, 94, 99*
Royal Doulton China: *30, 53, 54, 57, 119*
Linens by Orama's: *81*
Silver, china and crystal by Tiffany's: *81*
Flowers by Llewellyn Lyons and Madelyn Carey: *81*
Linens by Linen and Lace, *53, 54, 57, 119*

INNS AND B&Bs

The Inn at Fernbrook: *45, 46, 127, 128*
Grace Place Inn: *46, 64, 73*
Haderway House: *60, 61, 107, 123, 138, 140, 142, 143, 144*
The Mansion: *34, 35, 42, 75, 76, 79*